BRAIN SPARK

What kids deserve to know.

MICHAEL HARWOOD, M.D.
& ADRIAN HAMBURGER, M.D.

Brain Spark

Website: brainsparkbook.com

ISBN: 979-8-9851257-0-2

Front/Back Cover Design: Rob Williams
Caricatures/Cover Art: Elidor Kruja
Editing: Faisal Adeel
Logo Design: Olivia85

How to develop a brilliant mind!

In the age of the smartphone, where every little fact is just a few thumb swipes away, many would argue that the need to accumulate knowledge is no longer necessary.

We completely disagree. As parents and physicians, we have noticed that young adults are falling behind in terms of knowledge accumulation, while schools remain focused on reading comprehension and STEM.

Our goal is to cultivate the growing mind by introducing important people, concepts, places, and events. Many of these topics come up during adult conversations, during news events, or even online, and the eager mind feels left out.

Not only is knowledge accumulation critical to success in an increasingly competitive world, it also broadens all our horizons.

For optimal memory formation, we suggest that the book be read from front to back, one essay per day. In addition, we recommend you answer the sets of questions associated with that essay, as well as the ***Brain Spark*** questions – as those reflect on topics that are 1, 3, 7 and 14 days old.

Studies have shown that one of the keys to long-term memory is repeated exposure over short periods of time. This type of memory strategy is known as **spaced repetition.** Therefore, we have staggered these triggering ***Brain Spar***k questions to review and re-emphasize the key points (so if a question sounds familiar, that is on purpose!). This type of spaced repetition has been shown to help fully imbed knowledge into long term memory.

Important locations are also highlighted in bold. We recommend that, when you come upon each of the highlighted places, you take the time to find them on a world map. Awareness of geographical locations is another important part of developing a broad knowledge base.

Now, let's get started, and feel the ***Brain Spark!***

Table of Contents

STEVE JOBS

Who do we have to thank for the iPhone? The iPad? *Toy Story* and *Finding Nemo*? Well, we can thank a whole lot of people, but the simplest name to remember is **Steve Jobs**.

Steve Jobs grew up in California and dropped out of college to pursue his interest in computers. After working for the video game company Atari, Steve joined his friend **Steve Wozniak** in developing personal computers in their northern California garage. Together they created the **Apple** company in 1976.

From there, Steve Jobs became something of a phenomenon, and Apple battled other computer companies for dominance of the home computer market. Apple's **Macintosh**, a personal computer released in 1984, was a smashing success, and Steve Jobs became a household name.

Unfortunately, Steve's **confrontational** nature did not make him many friends and he was run out of his own company by 1986. However, that didn't stop Steve.

After his own failed attempt at a new computer company, Steve helped found and build **Pixar**. Pixar became the most successful animation studio in the world, producing a string of movie hits for decades (*Toy Story, Finding Nemo, The Incredibles, Monsters Inc.*, etc.). Pixar was later sold to the **Walt Disney Company**.

Without Steve Jobs, Apple was struggling as a company. Apple brought him back in 1997. Under Steve's leadership, Apple branched out from computers to personal music devices (the iPod), and eventually, to the development of the smartphone (the iPhone), perhaps the single most important advancement in our daily lives since the automobile.

Sadly, Steve died of pancreatic cancer in 2011. He left Apple as one of the biggest companies in the world, a **behemoth** now worth over two trillion dollars and a leader in **Silicon Valley** (California).

Interestingly, most photos of Steve Jobs today will show him wearing a black turtleneck and jeans. Jobs owned about 100 of the very same turtlenecks, all in black. The look of wearing the same outfit for every presentation was mimicked by other technology **entrepreneurs** including **Mark Zuckerberg** (Facebook), **Jensen Huang** (NVIDIA) and **Elizabeth Holmes** (Theranos).

Confrontational: someone who tends to deal with situations in an unfriendly, aggressive, and argumentative way.

Behemoth: something very large and powerful.

Entrepreneur: a person who risks their own money and time to create a successful business.

Silicon Valley: area in northern California near San Francisco that is home to some of the biggest tech companies in the world, as well as to the startups that hope to challenge those companies.

1. What was the name of the man who originally founded Apple with Steve Jobs?

2. Steve Jobs helped found and build which animation studio?

3. What is the name of the area in northern California near San Francisco that is home to some of the biggest tech companies?

4. What 1984 personal computer, developed by Steve Jobs and Apple, was a smashing success?

RASPUTIN

Before World War I, there was a very powerful **imperial** family in **Russia**: the **Romanovs**. The **Tsar** of Russia was **Nicholas II,** and the **Tsarina** was **Alexandra**. They had only one son, Alexei, who suffered from **hemophilia** and had a very sickly childhood.

The Tsarina found renewed hope for her son when she met Grigori Rasputin.

Rasputin was born in the 1860s in **Western Siberia**. In his twenties, he went on several **pilgrimages** to holy sites and came back a changed man. He started to preach and host private religious ceremonies. He eventually made his way to **St. Petersburg** (which was the capital of Russia until the **Russian Revolution** in 1917) where he became quite popular among many rich and connected families. It wasn't long before the Tsar and Tsarina met him and started hosting him at their palaces.

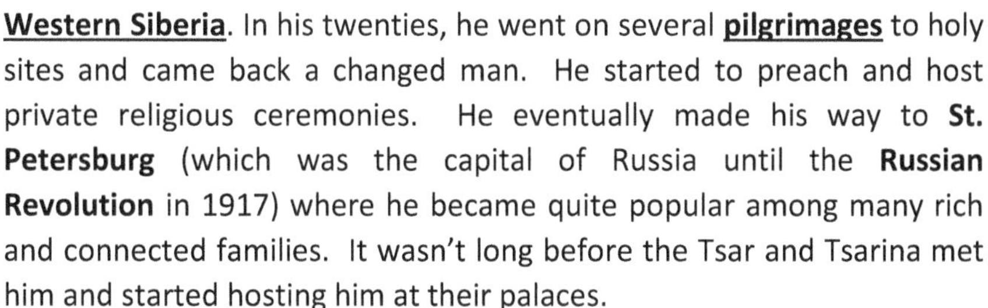

It is believed that in 1905 or 1906, he started treating Alexei's painful bleeding condition with prayer. For **inexplicable** reasons, Alexei's condition seemed to respond to Rasputin. This convinced the Tsarina to keep Rasputin around their family as much as possible.

As Rasputin became more involved with the imperial family, he started to feed advice to the Tsar and Tsarina. Unfortunately, a lot of this advice made things worse for the family, especially during a time of great struggle and unrest in Russia.

Some of the Tsar's family members and friends were so concerned about the control that Rasputin had over the Imperial family that they planned on murdering Rasputin. When Tsar Nicholas was away at the military front in 1916 (during **World War I**), Rasputin was lured to a prince's palace, and was offered his favorite pastries - but they were laced with poison! When Rasputin didn't seem to be affected by the pastries, they offered him poisoned wine. This didn't seem to hurt Rasputin either! At that point they shot Rasputin to death.

Many in Russia were very relieved to hear of Rasputin's murder, since he was seen as an evil influence on the imperial family. However, his death did not save the Romanov family. The entire family was murdered in 1918 during the Russian Revolution.

Hemophilia: a bleeding disorder where blood doesn't clot quickly enough. This can cause significant bleeding issues even with a small cut or bruise.

Imperial: relating to an empire or emperor.

Pilgrimage: a journey to a sacred or holy place.

Inexplicable: unable to be explained.

Tsar/Tsarina: emperor/empress.

Western Siberia: a desolate and cold region of Russia.

1. What was the name of the imperial family that was murdered during the Russian Revolution?

2. What word do Russians use to mean “emperor”?

3. What is the name of the bleeding condition from which Alexei Romanov suffered?

Brain Spark:

1. What is the name of the founder of Apple Computers, who also helped develop the Pixar movie studio?

OSAMA BIN LADEN

Osama Bin Laden grew up in a very wealthy **Muslim** family in **Saudi Arabia**. At the age of 22, after living in **Pakistan**, he moved to help **Afghanistan**'s resistance against invasion from the **Soviet Union**. In his twenties, he began to believe in a twisted philosophy of **jihad** that considered innocent women and children of the enemy to be a fair target. He was also convinced that the foreign policy of the United States was the cause of much harm to the Muslim world.

In 1988, Osama Bin Laden founded **Al-Qaeda**, an organization intended to fight against Jews and Christians who were perceived to be a threat to **Islam**. Al-Qaeda became a terrorist organization that helped launch bombings that injured and killed many civilians. The first big attack was in 1998 when truck bombs blew up in front of the U.S. **Embassies** in **Tanzania** and **Kenya** (both are countries in Eastern Africa).

Osama Bin Laden is most well-known for his organization of the **September 11th, 2001** suicide attacks on the **Twin Towers** in **New York City**. A group of Al-Qaeda terrorists boarded several flights, broke into the cockpits of those planes, and steered the planes into the two towering skyscrapers in New York City. They also flew a plane into the **Pentagon**, home to the U.S. Department of Defense in **Washington, D.C.** One of the planes, **United Flight 93** crashed into the ground in **Pennsylvania** when the passengers heroically fought the terrorists. Many thousands of people died that day.

This attack triggered an aggressive approach by the United States to get rid of Al-Qaeda and was the beginning of the U.S. invasion of Afghanistan, where it was believed that Osama Bin Laden was hiding.

Osama Bin Laden did in fact go into hiding but was eventually found to be living not too far from a military base in Pakistan. In 2011, the CIA and Navy Seals flew unannounced into Pakistan to arrest him. Bin Laden was shot to death during that operation.

Islam: a religion that believes that Allah is the sole God, and that Muhammad is his prophet.

Muslim: a person who follows Islam.

Jihad: a fight against the enemies of Islam.

Embassy: the headquarters of a government within the borders of another country. The United States has embassies within many other countries.

1. What is the name of the philosophy of aiming violence and war against the enemies of Islam?

2. Osama Bin Laden originally moved to Afghanistan in the 1980s to help fight against what invading nation?

3. On September 11, 2001, what Washington D.C. building, home to the U.S. Department of Defense, was hit by a hijacked plane?

4. In what country was Osama Bin Laden found and killed in 2011?

Brain Spark:

1. What was the last name of the Russian imperial family that hired Rasputin to heal their son?

DICK CHENEY

Did you know that many people consider that the most powerful man in the United States from 2001 to 2009 was in fact the vice president, and not the president?

Dick Cheney was vice president of the United States from 2001 to 2009 under the presidency of **George W. Bush**. He is thought of by many to have been the most powerful Vice President ever, because of his behind-the-scenes decision-making and the advice he provided to President Bush.

Dick Cheney was fascinated by politics. Although he dropped out of **Yale**, he did finish his degrees at the **University of Wyoming**. By the age of 28, he was working as an **intern** in Congress, and within five years he had worked his way up to becoming Special Assistant to U.S. President **Gerald Ford**. He then became the Chief of Staff to the President and President Ford's campaign manager in 1976.

When President Ford lost his re-election bid in 1976, Dick Cheney ran for the U.S. House of Representatives and became the congressman for the state of **Wyoming**.

In 1989, President **George H. W. Bush** (the father of the future President George W. Bush) chose him to become his **Secretary of**

Defense. He served in that capacity for four years and oversaw the invasion of **Panama** to remove dictator Manuel Noriega from power. He also managed **Operation Desert Storm**, the conflict that sent 500,000 U.S. soldiers and allied soldiers to help **liberate** **Kuwait** from **Iraq** in 1991.

In 2001, he became the Vice President of the United States. He played a very powerful role in that administration and is believed to have been the architect behind the 2003 invasion of Iraq to remove **Saddam Hussein** from power. As the Iraq war dragged on without any clear victory in sight, Dick Cheney became less and less popular.

He was also well known to have been a strong supporter of the CIA's **"enhanced interrogation"** strategies, which many saw as torture.

He **infamously** shot a friend in the face (by accident) while hunting in 2006. Thankfully his friend survived!

Intern: a person who works at a job in order to gain experience, sometimes without pay.

Liberate: to set a person, group, or country free from oppression or control.

Infamously: famous in a bad way.

1. Dick Cheney represented which state in the United States House of Representatives?
2. Under which President did Dick Cheney serve as Secretary of Defense?
3. In Operation Desert Storm, the United States went to war with Iraq in order to liberate which country?
4. The 2003 U.S. invasion of Iraq removed what Iraqi dictator from power?

Brain Spark:

1. Who was the leader of the Al-Qaeda terrorist organization until his death in 2011?

2. What state is Silicon Valley located in?

ARISTOTLE

Aristotle was a Greek **philosopher** who lived in the 3rd century B.C. He moved to **Athens, Greece** as a teenager and became a student of the famous philosopher **Plato**, who in turn was a student of the famous philosopher **Socrates**. After Plato passed away, Aristotle set up his own school called the **Lyceum**.

In addition to philosophy, he wrote and taught on many topics including **logic**, physics, **zoology**, **psychology**, economics and politics. In fact, his expertise on these subjects was so important that his writings were taught for the next 1,800 years, forming the foundation for much of our understanding of logic, philosophy and zoology.

One of his famous logic examples: All men are mortal. All Greeks are men. Therefore, all Greeks are mortal.

He also was the first person to study animals in a systematic way by using observation and **dissection**, making accurate conclusions that are still valid today.

When he was in his forties, he was chosen by **Philip of Macedonia** to become the personal tutor of Philip's son, **Alexander the Great**. He strongly encouraged Alexander's many conquests and also became the tutor to the future king of **Egypt** (Ptolemy) and the future king of Greece (Cassander).

After Alexander the Great died, Aristotle fled to a Greek island where he died a year later.

Philosophy: the study of knowledge, reality, meaning and existence.

Logic: the use of reason to come to conclusions based on specific rules or truths.

Zoology: the study of animals.

Psychology: the study of the mind.

Dissection: separation of something into pieces. This may refer to the actual separation of parts of a dead animal, as in science class, or the separation of a text or idea into smaller pieces to arrive at a more accurate conclusion.

1. In what city did Aristotle do much of his work?
2. What famous philosopher was Aristotle's teacher?
3. What famous philosopher was Plato's teacher?
4. What "great" king and conqueror was Aristotle's student?

Brain Spark:

1. Who was the U.S. vice president from 2001-2009, considered to be among the most powerful vice presidents ever?
2. At the end of which World War was the Romanov family executed?

FIDEL CASTRO

For the last five decades, American citizens could not travel to Cuba, or even buy Cuban goods. The reason behind this **boycott** was that the U.S. government was opposed to Fidel Castro's leadership.

Born in **Cuba** in 1926, Castro tried to become a politician in his early twenties. When the Cuban President cancelled the elections, Castro became more and more certain that the entire government of Cuba needed to be reshaped. Influenced by **communism**, Castro organized a **coup** and overthrew **President Fulgencio Batista's** government in 1959, placing himself in charge of the country.

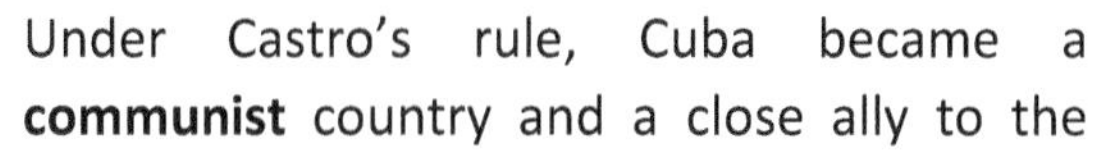

Under Castro's rule, Cuba became a **communist** country and a close ally to the **Soviet Union** (the biggest rival of the United States during the **Cold War**). Although Castro pursued the goal of making Cuba better for its citizens, he quickly undertook policies that had the opposite effect.

Castro and his government took over private businesses, restricted free speech and the press, and killed or imprisoned those who openly opposed them. As a result, many people, seeking to flee the **oppressive** country, risked their lives on rafts and floats trying to reach Florida (which is about 110 miles away). Many didn't survive the trip.

In 2008, after fifty years in power, Castro turned over the government to his brother Raul. Fidel Castro died two years later.

Communism: a political form of government in which all property is owned by the public, with the goal of eradicating social classes and making everyone equal.

Boycott: a punishment that forbids cooperation or trading with a country.

Cold War: a conflict without actual fighting, classically referring to the conflict between the United States and Soviet Union from 1947-1991.

Oppressive: making peoples' lives harder through cruel and unfair rules or laws.

1. What country did Fidel Castro rule as a dictator?
2. Who was the President of Cuba before Fidel Castro?
3. What type of government did Fidel Castro run: capitalist, communist, or socialist?
4. What was the name of Fidel Castro's brother, who took over power from Fidel in 2008?

Brain Spark:

1. What famous Greek philosopher was a student of Plato?
2. What country is the wealthy Bin Laden family from?

AL CAPONE

When the United States outlawed the production and sale of alcohol with the **18th Amendment** to the Constitution in 1919, many people hoped the **prohibition** of alcohol would lead to less crime and violence. They couldn't have been more wrong.

The era from 1920-1933 was known as **Prohibition**, when alcohol sales were made illegal. Unfortunately, when legal sales of alcohol were outlawed, gangsters stepped in and filled the void. Perhaps no gangster was more **notorious** than **Chicago**'s **Al Capone**.

Capone made most of his money **bootlegging**. A life of crime often comes with a large serving of violence. In order to eliminate other competing gangsters and to intimidate people, Capone was responsible for killing rival gangs. He organized the **St. Valentine's Day Massacre**, which involved his henchmen murdering seven rival gangsters.

Eventually, Capone was investigated by a group of honest detectives (known as "**The Untouchables"** since they refused to accept bribes) led by **Elliott Ness**. Although they could not legally pin any murders on

Capone, Ness's investigation did lead to Capone's arrest and **conviction** for not paying taxes.

He was sent to prison on the famous island of **Alcatraz**, located in the **San Francisco Bay** (California).

Prohibition was **repealed** in 1933 with the **21st Amendment** to the Constitution.

Bootlegging: making and selling alcohol illegally.

Prohibition: referring to the time in the United States when sale and production of alcohol was outlawed by the 18th Amendment, from 1920 to 1933.

Notorious: famous for being bad.

Convicted: found guilty of a crime by a court of law.

Repealed: to take back or cancel.

1. Which constitutional amendment outlawed the sale and production of alcohol in 1919, ushering in the era of Prohibition?

2. Which constitutional amendment repealed the 18th Amendment, re-opening the door for the legal production of alcohol in the U.S.?

3. What was the name of the infamous massacre ordered by Al Capone, killing seven rival gangsters?

4. Al Capone was sent to what famous island prison off the coast of San Francisco?

Brain Spark:

1. What Caribbean Island was taken over by Fidel Castro?

2. The 2003 Invasion of Iraq resulted in the removal of what Iraqi dictator from power?

RUTH BADER GINSBURG

The law can be very confusing! Lawyers learn the law, and judges help to decide how the law is interpreted. The most powerful and important judges in the United States are on the U.S. Supreme Court.

The **U.S. Supreme Court** is a group of nine judges appointed by the President and confirmed by the Senate for a lifetime of work. Ruth Bader Ginsburg was the 2nd woman to serve on the Supreme Court.

She started off studying at **Harvard Law School** and then transferred to **Columbia Law Schoo**l in New York City, where she graduated first in her class. She spent her life working towards gender equality and women's rights. In fact, she argued some of these cases in front of the Supreme Court as a lawyer. She was a very skilled lawyer, and instead of trying to remove all gender discrimination at once, she carefully chose her cases over time to successfully argue that gender **discrimination** had no place in the U.S. justice system or in the workplace.

She was chosen by **President Bill Clinton** in 1993 to join the U.S. Supreme Court. She became part of the so-called **liberal** wing of the Court, so named because they are the judges who often interpret laws with a liberal viewpoint. She was well known for her very forceful **dissents**. Her dissents were popular, and she was given the nickname "Notorious R.B.G.", which is based on her initials.

While on the Supreme Court, she wrote the **majority** opinion on some very important law cases regarding abortion, Native American rights and gender discrimination.

She was very friendly with Supreme Court Justice **Antonin Scalia**. This friendship surprised many since he was on the **conservative** wing of the court. They would often have dinner together and even go to the opera together.

She passed away in September 2020 after having fought through five different cancer battles over nearly 20 years.

Discrimination: unjust treatment of a group based on traits such as race, gender, or religion.

Liberal: in support of policies that favor the general welfare of society, social justice and a mixed economy.

Dissent: for the Supreme Court, a dissent is a formal disagreement with the winning ruling of the court.

Majority: for the Supreme Court, the majority refers to those justices who cast votes for the winning decision.

1. How many judges currently serve on the U.S. Supreme Court?

2. Which president chose Ruth Bader Ginsburg to serve on the Supreme Court?

3. Which conservative Supreme Court Justice was very good friends with the liberal Ruth Bader Ginsburg?

Brain Spark:

1. Who organized the St. Valentine's Day Massacre during the Prohibition era?
2. Aristotle served as the personal tutor of what great historical leader?
3. What was the name of the man who co-founded Apple with Steve Jobs?

JULIAN ASSANGE

If someone reveals government secrets, are they a villain or a hero?

That is the question surrounding Julian Assange, who originally founded the website **WikiLeaks** in 2006. This website would encourage **whistleblowers** to send in secrets from their workplace to be published online.

While some of the secrets published on Wikileaks did come from employees of large and powerful companies, the vast majority of secrets were sent in from employees of the U.S. government.

The most famous set of documents was released in 2010. **Chelsea Manning** was a U.S. Army soldier who worked as an intelligence analyst for the military. She had access to many top-secret databases and downloaded hundreds of thousands of documents (400,000 from the **Iraq War**, 91,000 from the **Afghanistan War**, and 250,000 diplomatic reports), sneaking them out of a military base on music CDs labeled "Lady Gaga". She initially wanted to send these to the **New York Time**s and the **Washington Post** but didn't get much of a response from them. She then sent all the documents to Wikileaks. This was one of the largest leaks of secret documents to the public.

This massive release of information, most of which was embarrassing to the United States, prompted the U.S. to investigate Wikileaks and, in turn, Julian Assange. The United States wanted the **United Kingdom** (where Assange was living at the time) to hand him over for charges of **espionage**. At about the same time, **Sweden** wanted to **extradite** him for charges of sexual assault. Assange claimed those charges were just another way for the Americans to get him out of the United Kingdom.

He went to the **Embassy of Ecuador** in **London** in 2012 and was given political **asylum**. He was allowed to stay in the Ecuadorian embassy. This protected him, as the UK police couldn't enter the embassy to make the arrest. Assange continued to coordinate the publication of more secrets on his Wikileaks website. Over the course of the next seven years, several countries continued to pressure the government of Ecuador to force Assange to leave the embassy. Eventually the Ecuadorian president decided that Assange had to leave, and Assange was arrested as soon as he stepped out of the Embassy in 2019. He is still in a UK prison.

To many governments, Assange is a villain who has revealed secrets that put other lives at risk. To many people, Assange is a hero for shining a light on the misbehaviors of governments and powerful people.

Whistleblower: person who reports, either to the police or the media, on the illegal or immoral activities of a person, group, or business.

Espionage: spying.

Extradite: to hand over a suspect or criminal to the state or country seeking to charge them with a crime.

Asylum: protection granted by one country to a person fleeing danger in another country.

1. What is the name of the website created by Julian Assange?

2. What was the name of Julian Assange's source for the largest transfer of government secrets?

3. What country provided asylum to Julian Assange in their embassy?

Brain Spark:

1. Which Supreme Court Justice is known by the acronym R.B.G.?
2. What was the name of Fidel Castro's brother, who took over for him as leader of Cuba in 2008?
3. What was the capital of Imperial Russia before the 1917 Bolshevik Revolution?

FREDERICK DOUGLASS

Frederick Douglass was born as a slave in 1818. As with many slave children, he was separated from his mother at a young age. He never met his father but was told that his father may have been a white slave owner.

He was transferred from one slave owner to another. At the age of 12, the wife of his master started to teach him the alphabet. He was very eager to learn, and within a short period of time he had taught himself how to read and write. Very quickly he started to teach other slaves how to read and write, which was very upsetting to the slave owners. The slave owners were convinced that educated slaves would rebel and leave the **plantations**.

After being whipped repeatedly and mercilessly by his next slave owner, Frederick Douglass escaped to New York City and eventually settled in **Massachusetts**. He became known as a preacher and as an **abolitionist**.

He became famous when he wrote his first autobiography in 1845 ***Narrative of the Life of Frederick Douglass, an American Slave***. This book was published several times, including in other languages for distribution around the world.

He gained more fame when he travelled to **England** and **Ireland**. He was amazed by the **integration** of Black people and white people in England and Ireland. While in England, he was able to sit in the same restaurants and in the same railroad cars as white people. In the United States, Black people were still **segregated** from white people, even in the anti-slavery states.

When he returned to the United States, he worked hard to spread his anti-slavery thoughts through his own newspaper. He also advocated for women's **suffrage** since he was convinced that all people should be treated equally regardless of color or gender.

In 1865, **President Abraham Lincoln** helped start the push for the **13th Amendment** to the constitution which effectively abolished slavery in the United States.

After the Civil War, Frederick Douglass was provided with more and more leadership opportunities within the U.S. government. He was recognized for his **oratory**. He was also the most photographed American of the 19th century, sitting for more portraits than even President Abraham Lincoln. He died unexpectedly from a heart attack at the age of 77.

Plantation: a large piece of property where crops, such as tobacco, are farmed by workers, often including slaves

Abolition: the act of ending a system or practice.

Integration: bringing together, particularly of races.

Segregation: the separation of races.

Suffrage: the right to vote.

Oratory: formally speaking in public.

1. What was the name of the famous book written by Frederick Douglass?

2. When was slavery abolished by the U.S. government?

3. Which U.S. constitutional amendment abolished slavery?

Brain Spark:

1. What was the name of the informant who provided the biggest government document leak to Wikileaks?

2. What crime did Al Capone commit that got him sent to jail?

3. What Washington, D.C. building was hit by an airplane during the September 11, 2001 terrorist attack?

GENGHIS KHAN

Did you know that one of the most powerful men in history was responsible for the death of roughly one out of every ten people on the planet?

Genghis Khan was one of the most powerful, and murderous, leaders ever. He was born in the 1150s (nobody knows for sure which year) and grew up in **Mongolia**, a country north of **China**. Genghis Khan is actually not his real name. He was known as **Temüjin**, but he was given the title of Genghis Khan, which is believed to mean either "supreme leader" or "leader of the sea".

At the time he was born, Asia was filled with warring tribes that were constantly attacking each other.

He rose to power by conquering various tribes and gained many followers because of how he ran his government. Soldiers would get promoted based on their achievements and not based on their family ties. Tribes that were conquered were not enslaved; instead, they were incorporated into his tribe. This approach gained him many followers and with every conquest he became more powerful.

One of the reasons behind his success conquering so much territory so quickly was his reliance on "Yam". This was a medieval version of the **Pony Express**, with waystations strategically placed throughout his empire. His riders could cover 200 miles in a day, allowing for rapid communication.

However, as he started to spread his empire outside of Mongolia into modern **China** and further west into **Persia** (modern day **Iran**), he became more **ruthless**. His armies would massacre the opposing armies, burn down villages and kill all the surviving members of any tribe that refused to immediately surrender. In fact, it is believed that his armies murdered close to three quarters of the Persian population. Overall, the world's population dropped by just over 10% due to his attacks.

At the time of his death in 1227, he had conquered most of Asia. His sons would further expand those conquests; they even made it all the way to Eastern Europe.

Pony Express: a 19th century American horseback mail delivery system.

Ruthless: showing no pity or compassion for others.

1. What medieval conqueror is believed to have led to the death of over 10% of the world's population at the time?
2. In what country did Genghis Khan grow up?
3. What was Genghis Khan's original name?

Brain Spark:

1. Who was the most photographed American of the 19th century?
2. How many justices serve on the U.S. Supreme Court?
3. Dick Cheney served in the U.S. House of Representatives as a representative for what state?

SITTING BULL

History is filled with proud warriors who stand up for themselves and their people. In the 1800s in the United States, many Native Americans were forced to defend themselves and their tribes against the U.S. Army. None is more famous than **Sitting Bull**.

Sitting Bull was a member of the **Lakota Sioux** tribe, located in **South Dakota**. As the American homesteaders and soldiers advanced into their territory, they forced Native American tribes onto **reservations,** thus allowing for the Americans to take more land. Sitting Bull was **vehemently** opposed to this and set up a camp for the Sioux tribe to defend their land.

The U.S Army underestimated these native warriors. In 1876, when famous **General George Custer** led his troops to force the tribes back onto a reservation at **Little Big Horn**, Sitting Bull led the Native Americans to a resounding victory. It would come to be known as **Custer's Last Stand**.

Waves of reinforcements of U.S. Army soldiers arrived and Sitting Bull was eventually forced to surrender and move to a reservation. In 1890, police tried to arrest Sitting Bull, as they (mistakenly) believed he was planning a revolt. A gunfight occurred at **Wounded Knee** and Sitting Bull was killed.

Reservation: an area of land that is governed by a Native American tribe under the U.S. Bureau of Indian Affairs.

Vehemently: in a forceful and passionate manner.

1. Sitting Bull was a member of what Native American tribe?
2. The Lakota Sioux were located in what state?
3. At what reservation did General Custer's "Last Stand" take place?
4. Where was Sitting Bull killed during a gunfight with U.S. Army soldiers?

<u>**Brain Spark**</u>:

1. What warlord had conquered most of Asia in the 13th century?
2. What country gave Julian Assange asylum in their embassy in London?
3. Aristotle was taught by Plato. Which famous philosopher taught Plato?

CHE GUEVARA

You probably have seen Che Guevara's face on t-shirts or posters, but never truly knew who he was.

Che Guevara was originally from **Argentina**, and he became most famous for helping **Fidel Castro** undertake a **coup d'état** in **Cuba** in order to install a **communist government**.

Guevara became a communist after spending years seeing the plight of poor people (while he was in medical school), but his tactics and beliefs were quite extreme. Rather than simply wanting to negotiate and pass laws, Guevara believed the only way to create a communist government was through violence and war.

Specifically, Guevara supported **guerrilla warfare**, a type of warfare where fighters are not part of a formal government army, and instead fight scattered battles against the actual government forces and police (and then retreat back into the woods or their villages).

After the *coup* in Cuba, Guevara helped lead armed rebellions in South America and Africa too, before being killed leading a revolution in **Bolivia**.

Today, Guevara is a controversial figure. His passion for revolution, and fighting for what he perceived was right, is celebrated by some. Yet many others see him as a villain, as he had a direct hand in so much death through his tactics. In addition, Fidel Castro's communist government, which Guevara helped institute and lead, ended up being responsible for the **persecution**, **oppression** and poverty of Cubans for decades.

Persecution: hostile or bad way of treating someone because of their political or religious beliefs.

Oppression: prolonged cruel and unfair treatment or control of a group of people.

Coup d'état: an illegal way of removing a government, usually by force.

Guerilla warfare: an irregular way of fighting, usually with small groups of fighters, using hit-and-run tactics against a larger better organized military.

1. In what country did Che Guevara help to organize a coup d'état in order to install a communist government?

2. What future President of Cuba did Che Guevara help come to power?

3. In what country was Che Guevara killed during another revolution?

Brain Spark:

1. The Lakota Sioux, Sitting Bull's tribe, were located in what U.S. state?

2. What countries did Frederick Douglass visit and notice that Black people and white people were better integrated compared to the United States at the time?

3. What type of government was instituted in Cuba by Fidel Castro?

ABBIE HOFFMAN

In the 1960s, the United States saw a lot of social unrest, with a lot of frustration focused on the prolonged **Vietnam War.** Anti-war **sentiment** became more and more common, as would protests against the government.

Abbie Hoffman was initially involved with the civil rights movement in the South, and then began to focus on anti-war protests and activities. In 1968, the **Democratic Party** had their national convention in **Chicago** so that they could select their next presidential nominee. Abbie Hoffman and others joined up in Chicago to encourage peaceful protests against the government (which at the time was run by Democrat President **Lyndon B. Johnson**).

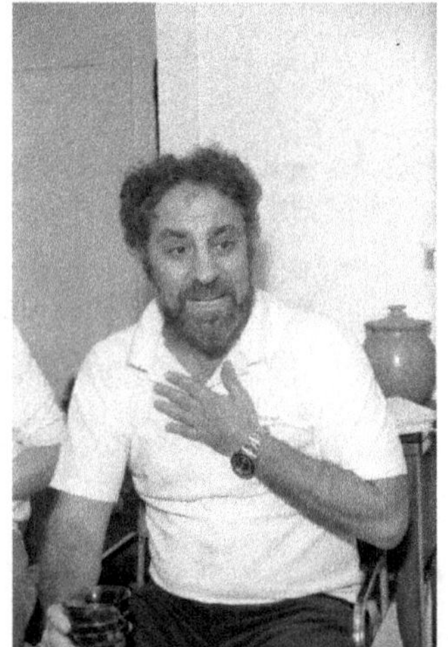

Chicago Mayor **Richard Daley** and the U.S. government had over 10,000 police and 12,000 soldiers prepared to face any protests or riots. There were several violent confrontations between the police and the protestors, with many getting injured.

Abbie Hoffman was one of the eight protestors arrested and put on trial for inciting the riots. One of the protestors had his trial declared a mistrial, and that left seven protestors. Those seven protestors became known as the **Chicago Seven**. They made many attempts during the trial to show that these charges were unconstitutional and would also frequently mistreat the judge by calling him names. Because of the behavior of the protestors during the trial, they were also charged with **contempt of court**. After they were all convicted, they filed appeals. The court's decision was reversed, and they were freed.

Abbie Hoffman's political movement was known as the **Yippie movement (Youth International Party)** with a focus on **harnessing** the youth in a political movement against the current culture. They would typically use pranks and comedy to make fun of the American culture that they disagreed with, including nominating a pig as the next president and naming that pig "Pigasus the Immortal". **"Flower Power"** was another anti-war, non-violent way of protesting with a focus on loving everyone and resisting the war, but quickly became associated with rock'n'roll, **psychedelic drugs**, and "making love, not war".

He remained an activist after the "Trial of the Chicago Seven", even though he was also aggressively pursued by the FBI and police for drug possession. He went into hiding for almost six years by leaving his family and changing his appearance before finally surrendering again to the police in 1980. He passed away in 1989 from an intentional drug overdose.

Psychedelic: producing hallucinations (the illegal drug LSD, for example).

Harnessing: to control and make use of something.

Contempt of court: the crime of being disrespectful of a court or judge.

Sentiment: an opinion.

1. What was the name of the political movement Abbie Hoffman belonged to that famously nominated a pig for president?

2. What was the nickname of the group of protestors that went on trial for inciting riots during the Democratic National Convention in 1968?

3. In what city was the Democratic National Convention held in 1968, a convention that sparked riots and violence?

Brain Spark:

1. What type of warfare did Che Guevara pursue in his revolutionary activity?
2. In what modern-day country did Genghis Khan grow up?
3. What "Untouchable" law enforcement official helped arrest Al Capone?

HENRY KISSINGER

Henry Kissinger was one of America's most famous **diplomats,** and one of the most influential people, of the 20th century. His impact on foreign policy during one of the most turbulent times in American history was monumental.

Kissinger grew up in Nazi Germany and was able to escape with his family to the U.S. in 1938. He finished school in New York City, joined the Army and eventually worked in military intelligence because of his German language skills. After World War II, he went to Harvard and went on to become a professor in the Department of Government at **Harvard.**

He joined **Richard Nixon's** presidential campaign. After Nixon won the U.S. presidency, Henry Kissinger was made the National Security Advisor to the President and eventually became the **Secretary of State** in 1973.

He is well known for his **"realpolitik"**, a German word which describes a system of politics based on power and practical realities instead of moral or ethical ideals. It means recognizing that the world can be mean and that sometimes you must make decisions that could upset some people, or even end up causing some bad things to happen.

He is most famous for three diplomatic achievements in the 1970s. He helped negotiate an end to the deeply unpopular **Vietnam War**. He started the relationship between the U.S. and **China** by setting up the first meeting between President Nixon and China's leader **Mao Zedong**. He also developed a policy of **"Detente"** towards the Soviet Union, which led to the first big agreement between the U.S. and the Soviet Union to reduce the number of nuclear missiles on each side.

Diplomat: a government official who represents his country abroad.

Detente: a French word that means easing relations between enemy countries.

1. Under what president did Henry Kissinger serve as Secretary of State?
2. What war did Kissinger help bring to an end?
3. Kissinger set up a meeting between Richard Nixon and what Chinese leader?
4. What was the name of the system of politics Kissinger used, involving uncomfortable decisions based on reality instead of pure ethics and morals?

Brain Spark:

1. What were the Chicago Seven protesting?
2. In 1876, Sitting Bull led the defeat of American forces led by what general?
3. Was Ruth Bader Ginsburg considered a liberal or a conservative Supreme Court Justice?
4. What was the name of the Apple personal computer released in 1984?

OSCAR WILDE

Today, when we think of funny people, we think of movie stars and YouTube personalities. However, at the end of the 19th century, one of the world's wittiest people was a **playwright** and author from Ireland.

Oscar Wilde was born in 1854 and began writing for a living in the 1880s. He was well liked for his sense of humor. In fact, he had a gift for witty sayings and an attention to life's interesting quirks. Wilde published his only novel, ***The Picture of Dorian Gray,*** in 1890. The novel has been a classic ever since, telling the story of a man who sells his soul in return for **immortality**, while a portrait of him ages and records his sins.

Wilde wrote two famous plays: ***Lady Windermere's Fan***, and his most successful masterpiece, ***The Importance of Being Earnest***. This was a classic comedy of errors where two men, hoping to put aside their boring lives, pretend to be a man named Earnest. While both are pretending to be the same person, trouble and **hilarity** happen when both become engaged to different women.

Wilde's growing popularity unfortunately made him a target of England's anti-homosexuality laws. Despite being married, Wilde was suspected of having romantic relationships with other men and was eventually jailed for this in 1895. He stayed in prison for two years, where his health deteriorated. Three years after being released, at the young age of 46, Wilde died of **meningitis**.

Both *The Importance of Being Earnest* and *The Picture of Dorian Gray* continue to live on in modern culture. Both have been adapted for television, stage, and cinema repeatedly over the past 100 years.

Among Wilde's most famous sayings are "Be yourself; everyone else is already taken" and "Always forgive your enemies; nothing annoys them so much."

Meningitis: an inflammation or infection of the lining of the brain or spinal cord.

Hilarity: extreme amusement, expressed by laughter.

Immortality: the ability to live forever.

Playwright: a person who writes plays.

1. What playwright and author was jailed under England's anti-homosexuality laws in 1895?

2. What is the name of the Oscar Wilde novel about a man who sells his soul so that he never ages?

3. What is the name of Oscar Wilde's most famous play, involving two men who pretend to be a man named Earnest?

Brain Spark:

1. What famous U.S. Diplomat used the phrase "realpolitik" when talking about dealing with the realities instead of the morals of negotiating with other countries?

2. What famous revolutionary helped Fidel Castro gain power in Cuba?

3. What was the name of the man who founded Wikileaks?

4. From what condition did Alexei Romanov suffer, causing him to easily bleed?

OLIVER CROMWELL

With the signing of the **Magna Carta** in **1215** (a document that limited the powers of the English king), England over the next 400 years saw a slowly weakening **monarchy** and a strengthening of **Parliament**. This back and forth between the English king (or queen) and the English Parliament eventually led to a Civil War in 1642. On one side you had the **"Roundheads"** fighting for Parliament, and on the other side the **"Cavaliers"** fighting for **King Charles I**.

At the time of the English Civil War, Oliver Cromwell was a parliamentarian, but he quickly became a military leader (without any military experience or training). He started off by commanding smaller units, and within two years was the second in command of the Roundheads due to his strong leadership skills and his uncanny ability to train his soldiers. By 1646, the Cavaliers lost, and King Charles I had to surrender. Parliament didn't know what to do with the King, and not long after, a second civil war broke out. At the end of this second civil war, Parliament and Oliver Cromwell decided that the King needed to be executed to stop any further civil wars.

England was now without a king, and Parliament wasn't quite sure how to manage the country and bring peace. Oliver Cromwell was chosen to run the country as **"Lord Protector"** and he fought more battles in

Ireland and Scotland to get rid of any resistance to his rule. He was especially harsh in Ireland, where many Catholics were murdered, and those that survived had their land taken from them.

He ruled England with an iron fist and believed that his leadership was inspired by God. Parliament even offered to make him the new King of England, which he declined in favor of remaining Lord Protector as he didn't want to establish a new monarchy.

He died at the age of 59 and his son took over the Lord Protectorship. His son didn't have the support of the military, and the country fell again into chaos. Parliament brought back the son of King Charles I, who they had just killed nine years earlier, and made him King Charles II.

The new King Charles promptly decided to have Oliver Cromwell's body dug up, his body hung up in chains and his decapitated head displayed on a pole outside of **Westminster Abbey** (a large cathedral near Parliament in London, England) for the next 25 years.

Monarchy: a form of government run by a monarch (king/queen or emperor/empress).

Parliament: a government body made up of individuals representing the people, making laws, and overseeing the government.

1. What 1215 English document was designed to lessen the power of the English monarchy?

2. What was the name of the supporters of Parliament in the English Civil War?

3. What was the name of the supporters of the king in the English Civil War?

4. What was the name of the king who was killed by followers of Oliver Cromwell after the second Civil War?

Brain Spark:

1. Oscar Wilde was a playwright from what country?

2. What war prompted the concept of "Flower power" in the U.S.?

3. Which constitutional amendment abolished slavery in the United States?

4. Osama Bin Laden originally moved to Afghanistan to help defend against an invasion by what country?

DIANA, PRINCESS OF WALES

So many children have dreams of princes and princesses, and the glorious lives that they lead. Who wouldn't want to live in a palace? Sometimes, however, that fairy tale does not have a fairy tale ending.

Diana Spencer was born in England in 1961. At the age of 19, she began dating **Prince Charles**, the **Prince of Wales** (heir apparent to the British monarchy). When the media found out about Diana and Charles, Diana's life changed forever. The **paparazzi** followed her and hounded her, and she became one of the most photographed and recognized people on the planet.

In 1981, Diana and Charles would get married in a wedding watched on television by over 750 million people worldwide. Princess Diana used her new position as Princess of Wales for good, bringing attention to world hunger, poverty, and the AIDS **epidemic**. She also had two sons, **Prince William and Prince Harry**.

Unfortunately, the fairy tale story had its troubles. Diana was quite unhappy, and in 1996, a divorce from Prince Charles was made official. That did not stop the attention. Even after Diana officially left the **House of Windsor** (as the British royal family is called), the press still followed her around. In 1997, while being chased by photographers, *Lady Di* was killed when her car crashed in **Paris, France**. She was only 36 years old.

Epidemic: a wide-spread infectious disease within a community.

Paparazzi: photographers who pursue celebrities, typically when the celebrities least expect it.

1. What was the full name of Princess Diana?
2. What prince did Diana Spencer marry?
3. What are the names of Princess Diana's two sons?
4. What is the name of the royal family of Great Britain?

<u>**Brain Spark**</u>:

1. What famous 1215 document limited the powers of the English king?
2. What famous U.S. diplomat set up the first meeting between U.S. President Nixon and China's leader Mao Zedong as a way of smoothing relationships between the two countries?
3. Genghis Khan developed a system known as "Yam", which is similar to what 19th Century American mail delivery service?
4. Under what president did Dick Cheney serve as Secretary of Defense?

COCO CHANEL

Coco Chanel revolutionized the fashion world of the early 20th century. She was born in **France** to very poor parents and grew up at times in an orphanage. She first attempted to make a career as a singer and performer but didn't find success. She pursued a career as a **seamstress**, learning how to sew dresses and make hats. She gained some fame in 1912, when a famous actress wore Chanel hats for her performances.

By 1913, with the financial support of her boyfriend at the time, she set up shops in Paris and in a fashionable area of Deauville (a village in northern France). Her clothes became quite popular as women became tired of the stiff, uncomfortable, hourglass shaped **corseted** dresses that were previously common. What helped propel her to stardom was the fact that she had made friends with rich and famous British and French **aristocrats**, all of whom would wear her dresses. Her outfits were more relaxed, much easier to put on and much more comfortable. Her shops generated so much profit, she no longer needed to rely on the financial support of boyfriends; she was wealthy in her own right. By the 1930s, she employed over 4,000 workers and owned multiple properties throughout France.

She also was quite famous for her perfume, **Chanel No. 5** (pronounced "Chanel Number 5"), which generated enough income for her to become one of the world's richest women at the time. She also famously designed the **"little black dress"** in the 1920s, which became very popular and was worn by women of all social classes.

When **World War II** broke out, she closed her shops and moved into the Hotel Ritz in **Paris**, where she became romantically linked to a German Nazi officer. It was even alleged that she was an **anti-Semite** and worked as an agent for the Nazi party. She moved to **Switzerland** after the end of World War II, as many suspected this was to avoid any charges in France for her activities during the war.

In 1954, she re-opened her fashion house, but control of the fashion label fell under the Wertheimer family (they were one of the original investors in the famous perfume). After Coco Chanel died in 1971, the fashion house struggled until the Wertheimers hired **Karl Lagerfeld** to start redesigning fashion for women. Lagerfeld was key to revitalizing Chanel and made it the success it is today.

Seamstress: a woman who sews for a living.

Aristocrats: a social class that a society considers its highest order, the upper class.

Corset: a supportive clothing that wraps around the abdomen, typically to create the appearance of a smaller waist.

Anti-Semite: someone who is hostile to Jewish people.

1. What is the name of the famous perfume made by Coco Chanel?

2. Coco Chanel was rumored to have helped which German political party during World War II?

3. What type of dress did Coco Chanel famously design in the 1920s?

4. What famous designer took over Chanel and made it the success it is today?

Brain Spark:

1. Fill in the blank: The modern day British royal family is known as "The House of ___________."
2. What Oscar Wilde novel tells the story of a man whose portrait ages him and reflects his sins, while he remains immortal?
3. What was the location of the battle that saw American forces, led by General George Custer, fall to Native American fighters?
4. Aristotle famously tutored Alexander the Great. What was the name of Alexander's famous father?

WOODWARD AND BERNSTEIN

One of the most important parts of a free and honest society is a free and honest media. The media can be an important check and balance to power and the abuse of power by government officials. There is perhaps no greater example of the important role of media than the work of **Bob Woodward and Carl Bernstein** during the 1970s.

Woodward and Bernstein were investigative reporters for the **Washington Post.** In 1972, there was a break-in at the **Watergate Hotel and Office Building** (pictured) in Washington, DC. This building wasn't just any building. It was the headquarters of the **Democratic National Committee**, which was in the midst of planning its **campaign** against Republican **President Richard Nixon** in 1972.

Woodward and Bernstein's investigation soon revealed that those involved in the burglary were linked to President Nixon's administration. The investigation, depending in large part on the inside information provided by a confidential source known by the code name "**Deep Throat"**, led to the unraveling of a conspiracy that led all the way to the president.

The scandal that followed, known as the **Watergate scandal**, led to 69 government officials being charged with crimes mostly related to burglary and **perjury**, and 48 being convicted. In addition, facing the threat of impeachment, Richard Nixon resigned the presidency in 1974.

The story of Woodward and Bernstein's reporting was recounted in the book *"**All the President's Men**",* which was made into a movie that earned seven Academy Award nominations and is listed in the top 100 greatest movies of all time by the American Film Institute.

Perjury: telling a lie to a court while under oath.

Campaign: an organized activity to win a political election.

1. What newspaper did Woodward and Bernstein work for?
2. What was the name of the scandal that Woodward and Bernstein investigated?
3. Which President was implicated in the Watergate scandal?
4. What was the name of the 1976 movie about Woodward and Bernstein?

Brain Spark:

1. What famous French fashion designer developed the "little black dress"?
2. Who was named "Lord Protector" of England in 1653?
3. Che Guevara was killed while leading a revolution in what country?
4. What was the term used to describe the "war without fighting" waged between the United States and the Soviet Union from 1947 to 1991?

HUGO CHAVEZ

The economy is a complicated thing! Sometimes, good intentions can result in disaster, especially when the government running the economy is not trustworthy. The story of Venezuela's socialist economy of the early 21st century serves as a warning of what can go wrong with a once promising economy.

Hugo Chavez was the President of **Venezuela** from 1999 to 2013.

He started his career as a military officer. While living in **Caracas** (the capital of Venezuela), he witnessed much poverty. He felt that the poverty was due to corruption and **capitalism**. He became a **socialist**. As he moved up the military ranks, he recruited soldiers and officers to follow his socialist ideals.

In 1992, the Venezuelan people started to riot against the government, and Hugo Chavez saw this as an opportunity to overthrow the government (a *coup*). His coup failed and he was imprisoned. However, the next president of Venezuela was friendly with Hugo Chavez and released him from jail in 1994, with the requirement that Chavez not return to the military.

Hugo Chavez travelled around Venezuela to promote his socialist views, which were very popular among the poor and the lower middle class. This led to his election as president in 1999. He pursued changes to the constitution in order to bring about a "Bolivarian" revolution (in honor of **Simon Bolivar**, a military leader from the early 19th century who had led several South American countries to independence from Spain). The constitutional changes provided more power to the presidency. He had developed the concept of "**Chavismo**", which was his brand of socialism.

At the time, Venezuela was the world's fifth largest producer of oil, which generated a lot of income for the country. Chavez used this money to build a lot of programs for the poor and to support other socialist or communist countries (such as communist Cuba). Chavez felt that he could make more money by having the PDVSA (the Venezuelan oil and gas company) take more and more control over other oil companies. He would also replace PDVSA workers with friends and supporters. Unfortunately, this led to the **corruption** of the PDVSA and the loss of a lot of expertise.

For a country that was so dependent on oil income, the collapse of the value of oil, combined with the worsening productivity at the PDVSA due to corruption, led to a worsening of the Venezuelan economy. Chavez's policies of creating price controls (so that food and supplies would remain cheap) and **nationalization** of companies ended up having the opposite effects; prices of food and goods skyrocketed.

Poverty and crime became a bigger issue in Venezuela, which threatened Chavez's role as president. However, he was able to make changes to the structure of government and promises to the poor that enabled his re-election to the presidency. He died from cancer in 2013, and his Vice-President **Nicolas Maduro** took over.

Corruption: dishonest behavior by those in power, typically involving bribery.

Nationalization: when a government takes over control and management of a private company.

Capitalism: economic system where the companies are owned by private owners (not the state) and motivated by profit.

Socialism: economic system where companies are owned or regulated by the community or the government, rather than private owners.

1. What country did Hugo Chavez become president of?
2. What type of political economy did Hugo Chavez implement in Venezuela: capitalist or socialist?
3. What natural resource was Venezuela's main valuable export, ruined by Hugo Chavez's socialist policies and corruption?
4. Who took over for Hugo Chavez as President of Venezuela in 2013?

<u>**Brain Spark**</u>:

1. Woodward and Bernstein were investigative reporters for what newspaper?
2. What are the names of the two prince sons of Princess Diana?
3. What was the name of the political movement led by Abbie Hoffman?
4. Al Capone ordered the murder of rival gangsters on what holiday in 1929?

ELON MUSK

Few people in the 21st century have had as significant an impact on business, technology, and the news as **Elon Musk**. One of the richest men in the world, Musk has repeatedly been in the news for his futuristic ideas and world changing companies.

Originally born in **South Africa**, Musk first became wealthy by starting a **software** company in 1995. He then joined **PayPal**, a company that allowed people to receive and send money online through the computer.

Today, Musk is best known for his leadership of the **Tesla** company. **Tesla** makes electric cars, with large batteries and electric motors, without having to rely on the moving parts seen in regular **combustion** engine cars. As the world grows more concerned about climate change and the environmental costs of **fossil fuels**, electric cars promise an opportunity for cheaper transportation that is friendlier to the environment. Tesla has also been on the forefront of developing a fully self-driving car, with the goal of eventually not needing an actual human driver.

Musk isn't just busy with electric cars. He had also founded **SpaceX** in 2002, a company that develops reusable rockets for space travel with the eventual goal of colonizing Mars. In 2016, Musk announced plans to use his new **Boring Company** (boring meaning "to create a hole", not "dull") to create super-fast tunnels in cities, including Los Angeles, for speedy travel.

While many would consider him a business **magnate** based on the success he has had with a variety of businesses, he prefers to consider himself a business magnet!

Magnate: a wealthy and influential business person.

Fossil Fuels: a natural fuel (oil, gas) that formed a long time ago from the remains of living organisms (trees, plants, animals, dinosaurs, etc.).

Combustion: the process of burning something. In combustion engines, gasoline is ignited to create pressure on pistons.

Software: programs that allow a computer to work or operate.

1. Where was Elon Musk born?

2. What company, designed to help people send money online via the computer, made Elon Musk a multi-millionaire?

3. What electric car company does Elon Musk manage?

4. Which of Elon Musk's companies was created with the ultimate goal of colonizing Mars?

Brain Spark:

1. Hugo Chavez was the president of what country?
2. What famous perfume was created by fashion designer Coco Chanel?
3. Henry Kissinger served as Secretary of State under which U.S. president?
4. Which U.S. president nominated Ruth Bader Ginsburg to a position on the Supreme Court in 1993?

SOCRATES

Today, social media is filled with people who love to argue! But perhaps no one mastered the art of argumentation better than Socrates.

Socrates is considered the father of Western philosophy and the first moral **philosopher**. He was a **Greek** philosopher who lived in the 5th century B.C.

Although he didn't write any books, he is best known through the writings of his students, especially **Plato**.

Socrates was popular among his students for using a specific type of questioning to determine the truth about a topic. It is now called the **Socratic Method**, which is a form of dialogue based on asking questions to encourage critical thinking, and to test underlying theories of thought. This form of questioning is still very popular in many law schools around the country.

As **Athens** was losing its strength in Ancient Greece, Socrates was clashing with the leadership of Athens about the direction of their government. He was sent to trial under charges of corrupting the youth of Athens with his teachings and philosophies. He was found guilty and was sentenced to death by drinking **hemlock** (a type of poison).

"Plato's dialogues" were written by Plato, focusing on the trial of Socrates. The most important part is Socrates's **"Apology"**, which in fact was his defense argument during his trial. Many of his defenses were based on human and political virtues.

Philosopher: someone who studies the nature of knowledge, reality and existence.

Hemlock: a tall flowering plant that is very poisonous. Chewing on six to eight leaves is enough to kill a grown man.

1. Who was the most famous student of Socrates?
2. What type of poison was Socrates forced to drink as punishment for "corrupting" the youth?
3. What book written by Plato focused on the trial of Socrates?

Brain Spark:

1. In what country was Elon Musk born?
2. What was the name of the scandal uncovered by Woodward and Bernstein, resulting in the end of Richard Nixon's presidency?
3. What was Oscar Wilde's most famous play, involving two men who pretend to be a man named Earnest?
4. What website, developed by Julian Assange, was created to leak secret information about large corporations and governments?

CHARLEMAGNE

In the **Middle Ages** (roughly 400 A.D. to 1500 A.D.), Europe was a ragtag collection of warring states and kingdoms. One particularly large group was known as the **Franks**, who lived in lands around what is today considered France (makes sense!).

The name **Charlemagne** comes from the Latin *Carolus Magnus*, which means Charles the Great. It is thought that he came from a wealthy and powerful family dating back to the end of the **Roman Empire**. He inherited the Kingdom of the Franks from his father **Pepin the Short** in 768 A.D. The Franks were a large **tribe**, located north of the Roman borders and spread out over what is currently France and Germany.

He invaded northern Italy and became **King of the Lombards** (the Lombards were the tribes of northern Italy). He became the protector of the pope and forced all his conquered people to convert to **Christianity** on penalty of death.

Pope Leo III crowned Charlemagne Emperor of the West in 800, and Charlemagne ruled over a united collection of states that would be known as the **Holy Roman Empire.** This empire lasted, through various forms, until 1806.

Charlemagne was not just a conqueror; he was a well-respected leader. After the Western Roman Empire had fallen apart in the mid-400s, most of Western Europe was in **chaos**. Charlemagne was able to restore order by setting up laws. He also encouraged the arts and literature. It was the beginning of the transition from the Dark Ages into the Middle Ages.

Chaos: complete disorder and confusion.

Tribe: a traditional community of families linked by religious or family ties, with a common language and culture.

1. What was the name of the large group of people who were led by Charlemagne?

2. What was the name of Charlemagne's father?

3. What religion did Charlemagne force his subjects to follow?

4. In 800, Pope Leo III crowned Charlemagne the Emperor of what empire that lasted about 1,000 years?

Brain Spark:

1. Which famous philosopher student of Socrates memorialized Socrates in his writings?

2. What failed economic system did Hugo Chavez implement in Venezuela: capitalism or socialism?

3. What English king was ousted from the throne prior to Oliver Cromwell coming to power?

4. The word "suffrage" refers to the right to do what?

IDI AMIN

Would you believe that one of the most powerful and brutal dictators of the 20th Century started his military career as an assistant cook?

Idi Amin was an uneducated assistant cook who rose through the ranks of the British Colonial Army. Within 20 years, he became the Commander of the Ugandan Army.

Uganda was under British control until it gained independence in 1962. When he was about to be arrested for misusing army money, Amin launched a **coup** and became President of Uganda in 1971.

While he was initially seen as being pro-Western, he quickly turned to other dictatorships and communist regimes for support. He took political prisoners and was responsible for the torture and execution of many of his prisoners.

During his presidency, his behaviors became more and more **erratic** and unusual. He gave himself a law degree. He claimed that he had beaten the British and gave himself the title of "Conqueror of the British

Empire". At one point he even declared that he was the last king of Scotland.

Within eight years of his rise to power, there was growing dissatisfaction with his presidency. He attempted an invasion of neighboring **Tanzania**, with the Tanzanian army counterattacking and taking over **Kampala** (the capital of Uganda). He fled first to **Libya**, then moved to **Saudi Arabia** where he lived in **exile**.

In 2006, a movie called ***The Last King of Scotland*** told the story of Idi Amin, with **Forest Whitaker** winning the Academy Award for Best Lead Actor for portraying the dictator.

Uganda: Where in Africa is it? It is a land-locked country between South Sudan, Kenya, Tanzania and the Democratic Republic of the Congo. It is close to the middle of the African continent.

Coup: when force is used to remove a government and replace it with a different leadership.

Erratic: unpredictable.

Exile: living away from your home country either by choice or because of a punishment.

1. Idi Amin was president of what African country?

2. In 1962, Uganda gained independence from what country?

3. What 2006 movie starring Forest Whitaker told the story of Idi Amin?

Brain Spark:

1. Who became King of the Franks in 768 A.D., inheriting the throne from his father, Pepin the Short?
2. What electric car company is run by Elon Musk?
3. What was the name of Princess Diana's husband?
4. What 13th century conqueror was responsible for the death of 10% of the world's population?

ANDREW CARNEGIE

Have you ever heard of a **philanthropist**? A philanthropist is someone who donates money to good causes in an attempt to make the world a better place. Philanthropists often have buildings, foundations and events named after them.

One of the earliest and most well-known philanthropists in American history was actually born poor in **Scotland**. **Andrew Carnegie immigrated** to the United States from Scotland in 1848 at the age of 13, settling in **Pennsylvania**. In need of money, Carnegie immediately started working. His work ethic was excellent, and he spent the next 15 years working different jobs and reading books. He loved learning.

In 1851, Carnegie began working for the railroad. His intelligence and work ethic paid off and he started making more money. However, rather than spend it, he wisely invested his money into other businesses, specifically iron manufacturing. By 1865, his labor and investments had created enough wealth to start his first company: a bridge and iron company. However, Carnegie soon realized that **steel**, not iron, was the future.

Carnegie began investing in steel by creating the Carnegie Steel Company. In 1901, this became **U.S. Steel**, which at the time went on to become the largest corporation in the world. Carnegie, a poor Scottish immigrant, had become one of the world's richest men.

However, Carnegie did not believe in just sitting on his money. He felt deeply about certain causes, which prompted Carnegie to become a philanthropist. His charitable giving has contributed to over 1,600 libraries, numerous schools, and foundations dedicated to world peace.

Carnegie Mellon University in **Pittsburgh, PA** is among the most prestigious universities in the United States. **Carnegie Hall** in New York is one of the premiere concert arenas in the world.

Pittsburgh is still known as the **Steel City**. The NFL's **Pittsburgh Steelers** owe their name in large part to the influences of Andrew Carnegie and the steel industry.

Philanthropist: a person who generously gives away money to help good causes (such as helping build a hospital, library or a university).

Immigrated: coming to live permanently in a foreign country.

1. In what country was Andrew Carnegie born?

2. What was the name of the steel company, led by Andrew Carnegie, which became the largest corporation in the world?

3. What university is named after Andrew Carnegie?

4. What city is now known as the Steel City?

Brain Spark:

1. Idi Amin became president of what African country in 1971?
2. What is the name of the "method" taught by Socrates as a way to determine truths about a subject?
3. What famous designer successfully turned around the fashion house of Chanel after years of struggles?
4. Where was Sitting Bull killed in 1890?

CHARLES LINDBERGH

Always fascinated with airplanes, Charles Lindbergh got his pilot's license in 1922 at the age of 20. He initially worked as a **barnstormer**, making money from performing airplane tricks for audiences around the country. By age 24, he was flying airmail routes delivering mail between **St. Louis** and **Chicago**.

Although flight was slowly becoming more popular, most flights were short distances due to challenges with weather and limited fuel. A few daring aviators had been able to cross the **Atlantic Ocean**, taking off from **Canada** and landing in **Ireland**. However, there was a prize for the first person who could fly from **New York to Paris**. Several famous pilots attempted this trip, but unfortunately lost their lives in the process.

At the age of 25, Charles Lindbergh flew the ***Spirit of St. Louis*** (a plane he helped design) in 1927, along with 450 gallons of fuel, to Paris. The trip took 33.5 hours, and he landed safely with crowds cheering him on. He became an instant celebrity, celebrated all over Europe and the United States.

In 1932, his one-year-old son was kidnapped and held for a $50,000 **ransom**. This became a national news story, and U.S. President **Herbert Hoover** offered the services of the FBI to help investigate this crime. Unfortunately, the boy was found dead not far from Mr. Lindbergh's home. Congress passed a law that year making kidnapping a federal crime. Within a year, the police tracked down the ransom money and found the suspected kidnapper. He was found guilty and sentenced to death.

Lindbergh moved to Europe in 1937 due to the unwelcome newspaper attention his family was getting in the U.S. Lindbergh was a staunch opponent of war, believing that the United States should not get involved in any further wars in Europe. This made him relatively unpopular with the military. Some thought that Lindbergh was pro-German and anti-Jewish, which further tarnished his reputation in the United States.

After World War II, he became an accomplished inventor. In fact, he developed some of the original equipment to help keep transplanted organs alive.

Barnstormer: someone who flies at airplane shows and performs stunts with their airplane. This was a popular form of entertainment in the 1920s.

Ransom: a sum of money to release someone held as a prisoner.

1. What was the name of Charles Lindbergh's plane?

2. Charles Lindbergh's famous flight across the Atlantic left New York and landed in what European city?

Brain Spark:

1. In what state did Andrew Carnegie settle after moving to the U.S. from Scotland?

2. Charlemagne forced all his conquered people to convert to what religion?

3. What was the nickname of the confidential informant used by Woodward and Bernstein to uncover the Watergate scandal?

4. What type of warfare refers to the tactic of using irregular fighting methods to defeat a more well-organized opponent?

MIKHAIL GORBACHEV

After World War II, the world lived in fear that the two global superpowers, the United States and the Soviet Union, may go to war. By the 1980s, perhaps the two most important individuals in the world were President Ronald Reagan of the United States, and Mikhail Gorbachev, the leader of the **Soviet Union**.

Mr. Gorbachev was the last leader of the Soviet Union. He was famously recognizable for a large red birthmark on his balding head. During the **Cold War** (1947-1991), there was a lot of tension between the United States and the Soviet Union. In fact, some would say that they were arch enemies. At the time, the only political party in the Soviet Union was the **Communist Party**, and Gorbachev quickly rose up the ranks and became a senior official by the late 1970s. In 1985, he was chosen by the **Politburo** (the highest-level committee that runs the Soviet government) to become the new

General Secretary (which is the term for leader of the Communist Party and therefore of the Soviet Union).

He was considered a reformist and was keen on **modernizing** the Soviet Union and improving its productivity. He promoted the concept of **"Perestroika"**, a term referring to the modernizing of the Soviet economy, making it more efficient. However, this eventually led to the Soviet Union realizing the limitations of **central planning** and moving away from the previous 50 years of Soviet central planning that had led to many inefficiencies and poor-quality products.

He then transitioned to **"Glasnost"**, which means openness. He was hoping that government transparency would lead to Soviet citizens becoming more informed participants in the economy. These changes allowed for more freedom of speech and made him more popular amongst the Soviet population.

In 1986, there was a failure at a large nuclear plant in **Chernobyl**. This was a catastrophe that further opened Gorbachev's eyes to governmental incompetence and poor workmanship, and he became more critical of previous Soviet Union decisions.

He also was involved in several meetings with U.S. President Ronald Reagan with the goal of reducing the number of nuclear weapons on each side.

As he tried to push through more reforms, more resistance was developing among hardline Soviet political leaders, which led to a coup in July 1990. They locked up Gorbachev and his wife at their country home and tried to take over the Soviet Union. However, this coup failed, and Gorbachev decided to start dismantling the Communist Party. This quickly led to the collapse of the Soviet Union. That wasn't his intention, as he had hoped to keep all the different states in an ongoing union.

Central Planning: a type of economy where the government decides what kinds of investments or products need to be made (instead of private owners and/or shareholders).

Modernizing: adopting new ideas or using new/modern equipment.

1. Mikhail Gorbachev was the leader of what superpower from 1985 to 1991?

2. What was the name of the bloodless conflict between the United States and the Soviet Union (a "war" that never had any actual fighting) from 1947 to 1991?

3. Which American president was responsible for many of the negotiations between the United States and Mikhail Gorbachev?

4. What was the Russian word for openness used to refer to the new policy of transparency in the Soviet Union under Gorbachev?

5. What nuclear power plant disaster occurred in 1985 and led to the deaths and sickness of many Soviet citizens?

<u>**Brain Spark**</u>:

1. What is the name of the plane Charles Lindbergh flew from New York to Paris in 1927?

2. What 2006 movie told the story of Idi Amin?

3. What term is used to describe the taking over of private businesses by the government (as was done in Venezuela under Hugo Chavez)?

4. Abbie Hoffman's arrest came as a result of riots and unrest at the Democratic National Convention in what city?

MALCOLM X

The fights for equality and civil rights are not always peaceful. Some people, like Martin Luther King Jr., advocated for peaceful methods to achieve justice. Others, like Malcolm X, believed that sometimes violence was necessary to bring about change.

The Civil Rights movement of the 1960s was an attempt to right racial wrongs and end racial injustice, **segregation** and racist laws primarily targeting African Americans in the United States, known collectively as **Jim Crow laws**.

Malcolm X converted to the **Muslim** faith while in prison in his twenties and joined the **Nation of Islam** (an American political and religious organization). He believed in Black empowerment, Black nationalism, and didn't support the concept of non-violence and racial integration that was encouraged by Martin Luther King Jr.

He became **disillusioned** with the strict rules of the Nation of Islam. He decided to leave that group so that he could focus further on political change for African Americans. He still advocated violence. He is famous for **"The Ballot or the Bullet"** speech where he encouraged African Americans to vote, but that if the U.S. government didn't allow African

Americans to gain full equality that it may be necessary for them to fight back with violence.

Sadly, in 1965, he was assassinated at the age of 39 by members of the Nation of Islam who had been unhappy about Malcolm X's criticisms of the Nation of Islam.

After his death, author **Alex Haley** published ***The Autobiography of Malcolm X***, based on conversations he had with Malcolm X. It became one of the most essential non-fiction books of the 20th Century.

Disillusioned: disappointed in something that turns out to be less good than one had believed.

Segregation: separating people based on the color of their skin.

1. What was the name of the set of racist laws that enforced racial segregation, particularly in the southern United States?

2. What was the name of the political and religious organization that Malcolm X joined, and later left, leading to his assassination in 1965?

3. What famous speech did Malcolm X give, encouraging African Americans to vote?

Brain Spark:

1. Who was the leader of the Soviet Union from 1985 to 1991?

2. Andrew Carnegie made his fortune from the production of what type of metal?

3. Elon Musk made some of his fortune by being a part of what popular internet payment company?

4. What Chinese leader met with Richard Nixon in a meeting set up by Henry Kissinger?

NELSON MANDELA

Many South Africans consider Nelson Mandela to be the "Father of the Nation", or **"Madiba"**, a respectful nickname given to older people in South Africa. He was a **transformative** politician who helped transition **South Africa** from Apartheid to an open multi-racial society.

Apartheid was a system of **institutionalized** racism that was based on white supremacy. It was established in South Africa in 1948, so that the minority white population could rule the country without Black population interference. Apartheid also made it illegal for white people to marry Black people. Over 3.5 million Black people were removed from their homes and moved to other parts of the country, since under Apartheid, race now determined where they could or couldn't live.

Nelson Mandela was born into a royal South African family in 1918 but was still relatively poor. He became very religious (Christian) and pursued an education with the goal of becoming a lawyer. He was very unhappy with the Apartheid system, and joined the **African National Congress**, a political party that was opposed to Apartheid.

He would travel around South Africa trying to gain further support for his movement against Apartheid, and tens of thousands would join the African National Congress movement.

The South African white government was very upset with this behavior, arrested him many times, and even had courts limit his ability to travel or to talk to people. Nelson Mandela developed an armed group to try to resist the Apartheid government with the goal of sabotaging government buildings. This allowed the government to arrest him for treason. He was sentenced to life in prison. He gave a very famous three-hour speech at his trial and ended that speech with "I am prepared to die".

He would spend the next 27 years in prison, including 18 years living in an 8 by 7-foot cell with only a straw mat to sleep on. During this time, he had become famous around the world. There were growing calls from world governments to stop Apartheid and to release Mandela from prison.

By the 1980s, South Africa was suffering financially from many countries refusing to do business with it on account of its Apartheid policies. South Africa was also very close to a violent civil war. The new President of South Africa, **Frederik de Klerk**, realizing the danger of a civil war, released Nelson Mandela (along with all other political prisoners) in 1990. This paved the way for national elections in 1994 and the end of Apartheid. Nelson Mandela's African National Congress party won the election and Mandela became the President of South Africa.

He worked hard to bring unity to the country. He also set up a "Truth and Reconciliation Committee" to investigate the crimes that happened during Apartheid so that South Africa could start moving on from its racist past. He served four years as president and then retired so that he could focus on his charity work. He passed away in 2013 at the age of 95.

In 1993, Mandela and Frederik de Klerk were awarded the **Nobel Peace Prize.**

Transformative: causing a big change.

Institutionalized: established as a common practice within a society.

1. What was the name of the system of racial segregation and institutional racism in South Africa?
2. What was the name of Nelson Mandela's political party that fought against Apartheid?
3. What South African president released Nelson Mandela in 1990?

Brain Spark:

1. What American religious and political organization did Malcolm X join?
2. What do we call performers that made money performing in air shows in the 1920s?
3. What was the name of the poison Socrates was forced to drink?
4. Fill in the blank of the title of Oscar Wilde's famous play: "Lady __________ Fan".

MARIE ANTOINETTE

Inequality is not new. In fact, the **French Revolution** of 1789-1799 famously came about as a result of inequality between the poor and the wealthy. Perhaps no one was a better symbol of inequality than Queen Marie Antoinette, remembered as one of the most controversial royal figures of her time.

Marie Antoinette was the daughter of the Empress of **Austria**. Austria and France had been enemies for a long time, and the Austrian Empress Maria Theresa (Marie Antoinette's mother) had hoped that a marriage between the two countries would bring about peace. Marie Antoinette was married to the future king of France **Louis XVI** at the age of 14.

She was not very well liked by the French nobles or the French people, primarily because she was Austrian. She was also unpopular because of the rumors that she was cheating on the King of France, and stories of her uncontrolled spending of money.

France at the time was in a lot of debt, further worsened by wars and the financial support of the 13 colonies during the **American**

Revolution. However, Marie Antoinette and her family continued to spend lavishly on palaces, clothes, jewelry and gambling.

The French people would print **"Libelles"**, which were little books slandering the monarchy by spreading quite vicious rumors about Marie Antoinette.

During her reign as Queen of France, there were several scandals that further hurt her reputation. The most famous scandal was the **"Affair of the Diamond Necklace"**. The former king of France, Louis XV, had a very expensive necklace made but died without ever paying for the necklace. Desperate to find someone to buy the necklace, a woman tricked a powerful man into believing that Marie Antoinette was in love with him. He paid for the necklace as a gift to the Queen. Instead, the woman took the necklace and stole the diamonds. Although it is likely that the Queen was not involved in this plot, the French people still suspected that she had something to do with it.

Later, as the peasants of France were starving, legend has it that Marie Antoinette was told that they had no bread to eat. According to the legend, she responded **"Let them eat cake"**. This occurrence, while likely not true, is a good example of how the peasants perceived Marie Antoinette to be out-of-touch and indifferent to their troubles.

During the French Revolution, the French people rose up against the rich and powerful. King Louis XVI was beheaded, and Marie Antoinette went on trial. She was found guilty of wasting money, **treason** and undermining the revolution. She was beheaded at the age of 37 in 1793 after a one-day trial.

In ***The Three Musketeers,*** author **Alexandre Dumas** relied on the story of "The Affair of the Diamond Necklace" as inspiration for his book.

XVI: roman numerals: X=10, V=5, and I=1. XVI means 16.

Libelles: little books, which were printed to spread rumors or lies in order to gain a political advantage. "Libel" is now an English legal term describing the use of written false statements in order to hurt someone's reputation.

Treason: the crime of betraying one's country.

1. What country was Marie Antoinette from?
2. What was the name of Marie Antoinette's husband?
3. What revolution resulted in Marie Antoinette being beheaded?
4. Legend has it that Marie Antoinette uttered what phrase when told that peasants had no bread to eat?

Brain Spark:

1. What was the name of the system of institutionalized racism operating in South Africa?
2. What is the Russian term for "modernizing of the Soviet Union" introduced by Mikhail Gorbachev?
3. What Pope crowned Charlemagne "Emperor of the West"?
4. Oliver Cromwell's head was displayed outside what famous London cathedral?

THURGOOD MARSHALL

The United States has a long history of racism, keeping Black Americans out of major roles in government for decades. So, it was a great step toward equality when, in 1967, the Supreme Court welcomed its first Black American **justice**.

Thurgood Marshall grew up in Maryland, where his father used to take him to watch court cases. They would then spend time debating the cases. Some believe this is the reason he eventually pursued a degree in law. He graduated first in his class from Howard University Law School in 1933.

For the next 25 years, he was closely affiliated with the civil rights organization known as the **NAACP (National Association for the Advancement of Colored People)** and argued many very important **civil rights** cases.

His most famous case was ***Brown v. Board of Education***. Previously, in 1896, the supreme court in ***Plessy v. Ferguson*** decided that it was okay to segregate Black and white Americans as long as they were treated equally. For example, a train could have a carriage for white people only and a carriage for Black people only, as long as they were going to the same destination. In other words, they were **"separate but equal"**.

In 1954, the Supreme Court agreed with Thurgood Marshall that you can't be separate AND equal at the same time, especially when it applies to public education. This was the big decision of ***Brown v. Board of Education***, finding that segregation in schools was **unconstitutional.**

In 1967, he was nominated by U.S. President Johnson, and then confirmed by the Senate as a Supreme Court Justice, becoming the first Black person to hold this position. Over the next 24 years, he built a strong record as a Justice who defended individual rights. He retired in 1991 due to poor health and passed away in 1993.

Civil rights: personal rights guaranteed by the U.S. constitution. Typically referring to protection from discrimination based on race, gender, skin color, sexual orientation, religion or disability.

Unconstitutional: not in accordance with the U.S. Constitution.

Justice: a life-long appointment by the U.S. President, and confirmed by the U.S. Senate, to the Supreme Court. One of nine justices who help determine whether a law is constitutional or not.

1. Who was the first Black Supreme Court Justice in the United States?

2. What U.S. President nominated Thurgood Marshall to the Supreme Court in 1967?

3. What infamous 1896 Supreme Court case found that "separate but equal" accommodations were legal?

4. What 1954 Supreme Court case reversed *Plessy vs. Ferguson* and found that segregated schools were unconstitutional?

Brain Spark:

1. What controversial French queen was beheaded in 1793 during the French Revolution?

2. Fill in the blanks of the name of Malcolm X's famous speech: "The __________ or the ____________".

3. What was the name of the infamous Ugandan dictator who ruled Uganda from 1971 to 1979?

4. What was the original last name of Princess Diana of Wales?

JOSEPH MCCARTHY

Have you ever heard of the term **"witch hunt"**? Originally this referred to the attacks on people suspected of being witches in the 1600s. More recently, the term "witch hunt" is used to describe instances where people have been unfairly and ruthlessly attacked and persecuted for beliefs or actions that are not actually illegal but are deemed "dangerous" by some members of society.

There is perhaps no greater modern example of a "witch hunt" than the rise of Joseph McCarthy in the 1950s. Joseph McCarthy was a United States Senator from **Wisconsin**. In 1950, he began an aggressive campaign of accusations against certain Americans, claiming that they were **communists**.

In the 1950s, the **Cold War** (a "war" of tension but no actual armed fighting) between the United States and the **Soviet Union** created great worry throughout both countries. In the United States, some were worried that the country would be overrun by people **sympathetic** to the Soviet form of government known as communism. Soon, people began accusing others of being communists. While these accusations were sometimes true and sometimes not true, it is important to remember that in a free country like America, it is not a crime to have unpopular beliefs.

However, with accusations of communism came the loss of jobs and opportunities, known as "**blacklisting**". For instance, people in Hollywood could not get jobs if they were suspected of being communists.

The "witch hunt" for communists reached its peak with Joseph McCarthy. McCarthy made reckless claims, often without evidence, and ruined lives. It became clear to many that while protecting against Soviet **infiltration** was important, McCarthy was taking it too far. His fellow Senators began to distance themselves from him.

In 1954, when McCarthy brought accusations against the U.S. Army, a nationally televised hearing saw attorney **Joseph Welch** challenge McCarthy. His statement "You have done enough. **Have you no sense of decency**?" seemed to strike a chord with the American public that Senator McCarthy was going too far.

His popularity collapsed. He was **censured** by his fellow Senators and lost their respect. He died four years later, largely ignored.

Censure: an official statement of disapproval.

Infiltration: gaining access to something in a secret/stealthy manner.

Sympathetic: sharing a common feeling.

Communism: a system of government wherein all property is shared by everyone instead of by individuals, and therefore economic and business decisions are decided by the government, not the citizens.

1. Joseph McCarthy was a U.S. Senator from which state?

2. The tactic of restricting job opportunities from people with certain unpopular beliefs (such as communism) is known by what "colorful" word?

3. Joseph McCarthy's witch hunt was designed to find, and persecute, people who supported what form of government?

4. What was the name of the attorney who asked Joseph McCarthy "Have you no sense of decency?" on national television?

Brain Spark:

1. Who was the first Black Supreme Court Justice of the United States?

2. What was the name of Nelson Mandela's political party?

3. What Pittsburgh, PA university was originally established by Andrew Carnegie in 1900?

4. During World War II, Coco Chanel was rumored to be supportive of what German political party?

ELIZABETH HOLMES

Do you know what the **"cult of personality**" is? It refers to the ability of certain people to convince others to join them, not through logic and reason, but by using their personality to appeal to people's emotions. While the term generally refers to political leaders, fraudsters and con artists commonly trick well-meaning and intelligent people into believing the impossible, and then escape with fame and fortune, leaving the poor victim behind.

Elizabeth Holmes seemingly came out of nowhere to dominate the business and technology world. Holmes created the company **Theranos**, which she claimed possessed a technology that could run hundreds of blood tests from just a drop of blood. The technology was deemed to be impossible by people in the medical and technology fields. Yet Holmes, who had minimal formal training in either field, was able to convince powerful and very wealthy people to support her business, to promote her as a business woman, and to pour hundreds of millions of dollars into Theranos.

Soon, Theranos partnered with **Walgreens**, a huge chain of pharmacies. By 2015, Theranos was valued at $9 billion. Elizabeth Holmes was now a self-made billionaire.

There was one problem. The technology Theranos was promising did not exist as she claimed. Instead, Holmes and Theranos allegedly used lies and legal threats to cover up the reality that their technology was not what she was promising. In 2015, John Carreyrou of the ***Wall Street Journal*** published an article detailing the truth about Theranos. Elizabeth Holmes's fall from grace was rapid.

Within a few years, Theranos ceased all operations, going from a business worth $9 billion to a business worth nothing. Elizabeth Holmes, meanwhile, was charged with **fraud** and **conspiracy**.

How can so many seemingly brilliant and successful people be swayed by someone who is lying and manipulating? How could so many **titans of industry** give money to a person who was lying about what her technology could or could not do? The answer is the power of "personality". The truth is we are all capable of being **duped** by slick people. It is always important to make sure we look at logic, data, and reason, and not trust people simply because they tell us what we want to hear.

Fraud: criminally lying or deceiving somebody for personal or financial gain.

Titan of industry: a very important and powerful person in that field.

Duped: deceived or tricked.

Conspiracy: a secret plan by a group of people to do something harmful.

1. What was the name of the woman who created Theranos, a company falsely claiming to be able to run hundreds of blood tests from a single drop of blood?

2. What was the name of the company Elizabeth Holmes founded, that went from being worth billions to losing all of its value?

3. What large pharmacy chain was duped into partnering with Theranos?

Brain Spark:

1. What 1950s American senator became iconic for his aggressive witch hunts, attempting to uncover communists in America?
2. Marie Antoinette was married to what French king?
3. What aviator's baby was famously kidnapped in 1932?
4. What movie starred Dustin Hoffman and Robert Redford in the roles of Woodward and Bernstein?

DOUGLAS MACARTHUR

"I'll be back." That line was famously uttered by Arnold Schwarzenegger in the 1984 film ***The Terminator***. 42 years earlier, a U.S. Army General uttered a similar phrase: "I shall return", as a promise to win a war.

Starting in 1939, **World War II** lasted six bloody years, when the Allied armies finally defeated the Axis forces of **Germany and Japan**.

One of the most important figures in the victory of the **Allies** over Japan was **General Douglas MacArthur.** Like many generals at the time, MacArthur had studied at the **United States Military Academy at West Point, New York**. He made a name for himself fighting in World War I.

As World War II began to **brew** in Asia and Europe, MacArthur was put in charge of U.S. forces in the **Pacific Ocean**. After Japan launched their surprise attack on **Pearl Harbor** in **Hawaii**, the Japanese set their sights on attacking the **Philippines.** General MacArthur had to escape the Philippines in 1942, but he famously proclaimed, **"I shall return."**

Return he did! MacArthur gathered forces and returned to the Philippines, repeatedly defeating Japanese forces and turning the **tide**

of the war. The Allies ultimately won World War II, and MacArthur was a hero. He helped rebuild Japan, which had been so severely damaged in the war.

When the United States entered the **Korean War** in 1950, MacArthur was again named commander. This time his job was to protect South Korea from North Korean invaders. However, after a disagreement with **U.S. President Harry Truman** about the war plans, he was fired.

Brew: to bring about.

Tide of War: just like the ocean tides, the tides of war can switch direction.

Allies: coalition of countries that battled Germany and Japan in World War II.

1. What was the name given to the forces that battled Germany and Japan in World War II?
2. The United States entered World War II after Japan surprised them with an attack on what base in Hawaii?
3. What country did General Douglas MacArthur escape from in 1942, vowing "I shall return"?
4. General Douglas MacArthur was fired as commander of the Korean War by which U.S. President?

Brain Spark:

1. What was the name of the blood testing company founded by Elizabeth Holmes?

2. What Supreme Court case originally decided that it was okay to separate people based on their skin color as long as the accommodations provided were equal (the idea of "separate but equal")?

3. Meaning "openness", what was the name of Gorbachev's policy that allowed for more open and honest communication between the Soviet government and its citizens?

4. What was the name of the person who replaced Hugo Chavez as leader of Venezuela?

AYATOLLAH KHOMEINI

People often use religion and faith to promote peace and love. Others sadly use religion as a powerful tool to oppress others. Iranian Supreme Leader Ayatollah Khomeini was one such controversial leader. His government remained popular among many devout Muslim Iranians, while at the same time oppressing homosexuals, women and imprisoning or murdering political opponents.

Until 1979, **Iran** (formerly known as **Persia**) was run by a **shah** (king). The Iranian Revolution of 1979 brought Ayatollah Khomeini into power, sending the Shah of Iran into **exile**.

Ayatollah Khomeini grew up studying the **Quran** (Islam's holy book). He went into exile for 15 years from Iran in opposition to the shah. He returned to Iran in 1979 to help overthrow the shah. He strongly believed that the country should be run by Islamic **jurists** in accordance with Islamic law **(Sharia)**. He quickly established himself as the Guardian of the law, and thus became the **Supreme Leader of Iran.**

He called the United States the "Great Satan". He supported the taking of 52 U.S. hostages for 444 days (1979 to 1980) after the U.S government allowed the former shah to receive medical treatment in the United States.

Because of the instability in Iran shortly after the shah left, **Iraq** (under **Saddam Hussein**) decided to invade Iran in order to control some oil rich areas. This led to the eight-year Iran-Iraq War. It was a particularly brutal war because of Saddam Hussein's use of chemical weapons. This war occupied much of Khomeini's reign as Supreme Leader. Within a year of the war ending in 1988, Khomeini died at the age of 89 from several heart attacks.

He is also well known for issuing a **fatwa** (a ruling from authority) for the death of **Salman Rushdie**. Salman Rushdie had written a book called ***The Satanic Verses***, which was seen as **blasphemous** by many Muslims.

Blasphemous: saying or doing something against God.

Exile: being barred from your home country either for political reasons or as a punishment.

Jurist: an expert in law, either a lawyer or a judge.

1. Ayatollah Khomeini was the Supreme Leader of what country?

2. What was the previous name of Iran?

3. What was the name of the Iraqi President who invaded Iran in 1980?

4. Salman Rushdie had to go into hiding after Ayatollah Khomeini issued a "fatwa" for his death after writing what novel?

Brain Spark:

1. What U.S. general famously proclaimed "I shall return" after his forces were driven out of the Philippines during World War II?

2. Senator Joseph McCarthy served in the U.S. Senate representing what U.S. state?

3. What author published *The Autobiography of Malcolm X?*

4. What is the name of the space travel company founded by Elon Musk?

YASSER ARAFAT

For many years, Israel and Palestine have been in conflict, a conflict that continues right up to the publishing of this book! It is a conflict that can be confusing, especially when you realize that the State of Palestine is not recognized as an official state by Israel or the United States, and you won't find it on some maps!

Yasser Arafat was the leader of the **Palestinian Liberation Organization (PLO)**, the ruling government of the State of Palestine.

Palestine is the area that covers **Israel**, the **West Bank** and **Gaza**, and has been an area that has been strongly **contested** over the last 2,000 years by different religions (Christianity, Judaism and Islam) as well as different countries. When the state of Israel was created in 1948, this triggered multiple wars between Israel and its surrounding Arab neighbors. Over time, more and more Palestinians had to leave their ancestral homes and move into the Gaza Strip or into the West Bank, or into refugee camps in neighboring **Lebanon** and **Jordan**.

Although Yasser Arafat grew up in Egypt, his parents were Palestinian, and he considered himself Palestinian as well. He became an **anti-Zionist** and participated in the 1948 **Israel-Arab War** on the Arab side.

Yasser Arafat helped found the **Fatah movement**. This was a political movement for the **liberation** of Palestine, which was also known for having members that participated in terrorist activities. Over the next 50 years, Yasser Arafat relied on politics to gain the support of other Arab countries (most of which were opposed to Israel). He also used terrorist activities to attack Israelis within the state of Israel and elsewhere. In fact, he is suspected to have been linked to many terrorist acts including the murder of 11 Israeli athletes at the Summer Olympics in **Munich, Germany.**

Israel responded harshly to each and every attack by the PLO. Israel ramped up the counterattacks, arrested more PLO members, and even made several attempts to assassinate Arafat.

By the mid-1990s, Arafat decided to openly abandon terrorism in return for negotiations with Israel to bring peace to the region. This led to the 1993 **Oslo Accords** between Israel, the PLO and the United States. This peace deal led to the PLO officially recognizing Israel, and Israel offering for the PLO to self-govern its territories in Gaza and the West Bank. These groundbreaking peace agreements led to Yasser Arafat sharing the Nobel Peace Prize in 1994 with Israel's leaders (Shimon Peres and Yitzhak Rabin).

He died in 2004 as a controversial figure in the Middle East. The United States and Israel considered him an unreliable politician. The Palestinian people saw him as an unrelenting leader.

Anti-Zionist: someone who is opposed to the establishment of a Jewish State in Israel.

Liberation: the act of setting someone or some country free from imprisonment or control.

Contested: argued over.

1. What was the name of the official government of the State of Palestine?
2. What was the name of the movement for the liberation of Palestine?
3. The 1972 Summer Olympics, which saw the murder of 11 Israeli athletes, was held in which city?
4. What was the name of the 1993 peace agreement between Israel, Palestine, and the United States?

<u>**Brain Spark**</u>:

1. What Iranian became the Supreme Leader of Iran after overthrowing the shah?
2. What is the name of the founder of Theranos? She was charged with fraud after her business was alleged to have lied to investors and the public about its capabilities.
3. What South African was imprisoned for 27 years for fighting to end Apartheid?
4. Which of Plato's writings focused on Socrates's trial?

GOLDA MEIR

Golda Meir was the first (and only) female Prime Minister of Israel.

She was born in the Ukraine in 1898. She moved with her family to **Wisconsin** in the United States in 1906 when she was eight years old. She quickly showed her leadership skills as a student, even holding fundraisers to help pay for textbooks at school.

Golda left her home and moved in with her older sister in **Denver, Colorado**. There she was exposed to many discussions about Zionism, socialism, labor unions and women's **suffrage**. **Zionism** is the belief that a Jewish state should be established and maintained in **Israel**. Women's suffrage is the right for women to vote in elections.

When she got married in 1917, she decided that she would move to the British controlled **Palestine** as soon as possible (the British controlled the area from 1920 to 1948). This move was delayed by World War I. She finally made it to Palestine in 1921. Once there, she joined a **kibbutz** (a socialist and Zionist community that focuses on working together to work the land and produce fruits and vegetables).

She quickly became very involved in politics and worked her way up to become the acting head of the political department of the Jewish Agency in British Palestine. She worked very hard (along with other Zionists) to help establish the state of Israel after the atrocities of World War II. During World War II, Nazis murdered over six million Jews, and most countries around the world refused to take Jewish refugees from that war.

She knew that the surrounding **Arab** states would likely attack the newly formed Israel right away. She travelled to the United States and raised over $50 million to help buy weapons and arms to help protect Israel from any attacks. She had planned well, since the Arab states did in fact try to invade Israel. The Israelis were able to win that first war in 1948.

She was immensely popular in Israel. She was elected Prime Minister in 1969, staying in that role for five years. She was devastated when Israeli Olympic athletes were taken hostage and executed by Palestinian terrorists during the **1972 Olympic Games** in **Munich, Germany.** She authorized the **Mossad** (the Israeli intelligence agency) to track down the terrorists and assassinate them. She was getting old and tired of the burden she was carrying and resigned in 1974 (despite remaining quite popular in Israel). She passed away from cancer in 1978.

Suffrage: the right to vote in a political election.

Zionism: the political movement to develop and maintain a Jewish State in what is now Israel.

1. Who was the first female Prime Minister of Israel?

2. In what year were the Olympic games marred by the murder of Israeli athletes at the hands of Palestinian terrorists?

3. What is the name of the Israeli intelligence agency?

Brain Spark:

1. Yasser Arafat served as the leader of what organization, considered the government of the State of Palestine?
2. What war did General Douglas MacArthur participate in from 1950 until being fired in 1953?
3. Marie Antoinette was the daughter of the empress of what country?
4. From 800 to 813, Charlemagne ruled over a collection of states known collectively as what?

NERO

Someday, you will hear: "**Nero fiddled, while Rome burned**." What does this mean? Who was Nero?

Nero was **emperor** of the **Roman Empire** from 54 A.D. to 68 A.D. At the time, the Roman Empire was the supreme power in Europe. He was only 17 when he took the throne. As the years of his reign passed, he became more and more of a **tyrant**. He killed his **opponents** and critics. He also spent the empire's money lavishly on his own interests, including large parties, his art collection, and his own musical interests.

In 64 A.D., a large part of Rome was engulfed in flames, lasting over a week. The rumors of the time suggested that Nero played a **fiddle** (or a **lyre**) while he watched the city burn, and that he blamed others (especially Christians) for starting the fires. Some of his opponents suggested that perhaps Nero set the fire himself so that he could expand his palace.

Nero's reign ended in 68 A.D. when he instructed his private secretary to kill him, as Nero was afraid that his enemies were beginning to revolt against him.

Tyrant: a cruel ruler.

Lyre: a small harp-like instrument.

Opponent: a challenger or rival.

1. What empire was the supreme power in Europe in the 1st century A.D.?
2. Who was the Emperor of Rome from 54-68 A.D.?
3. Rumor has it that Nero played what instrument "while Rome burned"?

Brain Spark:

1. Golda Meir was the first female Prime Minister of what country?
2. Prior to the rule of Ayatollah Khomeini, Iran was run by a king, called by what Persian word?
3. Thurgood Marshall was closely affiliated with what civil rights organization?
4. What is the capital of Uganda?

LOUIS PASTEUR

Louis Pasteur was a French scientist in the 1800s. Although not a great student in his teenage years, he became more focused on **chemistry** and **physics** by his early twenties.

He made several **momentous** discoveries in chemistry, including the fact that some chemicals are right-handed or left-handed based on how they twist light going through them.

He was able to disprove most scientists of the time who believed that germs came out of nowhere. He was also able to prove that germs can move around and generate more germs. Because of this, he is known as the father of **"Germ Theory"**.

In fact, he realized that heat could **sterilize** germs and used that technique to get rid of bacteria and molds in milk. This process of heating a liquid to kill germs is called "**pasteurization**" and is still used to this day for most liquids that you buy at the store (including canned foods and even eggs). He started to encourage doctors to wash their hands and instruments in hot water to reduce infections during surgery.

He discovered that weakened viruses/germs could be used to vaccinate animals and people. He was also the first to develop the vaccine for **rabies**. At that time, being bitten by a **rabid** animal would mean a painful death within a few days to a week. People from all over the world who had been bitten would travel to Paris to be cured by Louis Pasteur. This prompted him to set up the **Pasteur Institute** in France in 1887. This institute has been at the forefront of **microbiology** ever since. The Pasteur Institute has led to the control of many terrible diseases including **tetanus**, **polio**, **influenza**, and the **plague**.

Microbiology: the study of germs

Momentous: of great significance or importance.

Sterilize: make something free from germs. It can also mean removing the ability to have off-spring.

Rabid: an animal affected by rabies. Rabies is a very contagious and fatal virus that can cause madness and convulsions, typically transmitted through saliva.

Tetanus: a bacterial disease that leads to stiffening and cramping of muscles, sometimes interfering with the ability to breathe.

Polio: a viral disease that can lead to temporary or even permanent paralysis of the body.

Influenza: a viral infection that can impact the lungs, causing fevers and body aches.

Plague: a contagious bacterial disease that leads to fevers and can be deadly.

1. Louis Pasteur is considered the father of what "theory" of disease?

2. What is the name of the sterilization process invented by Louis Pasteur and still used to kill bacteria in milk?

3. Louis Pasteur developed the first vaccine for what deadly disease?

4. What is the name of the foundation in France set up by Louis Pasteur and which has been at the forefront of advances in microbiology for over a century?

Brain Spark:

1. Who was the emperor of the Roman Empire during the Great Fire of Rome in 64 A.D.?

2. What was the name of the 1993 agreements between Palestine, the U.S. and Israel, that ultimately earned Yasser Arafat the Nobel Peace Prize?

3. What is the colorful term used to describe how suspected communists were put on a "list" of people who could not be hired for jobs?

4. What is the nickname of Pittsburgh, Pennsylvania?

CHARLES DE GAULLE

The most famous French figure of the 19th century, **Napoleon Bonaparte**, was only 5 feet and 6 inches tall. In the 20th century, however, France was famously led by a very tall man with a commanding presence.

Also known as the **"Great Asparagus"**, Charles de Gaulle was 6 foot 5 inches, had a tall forehead and a big nose, and spent much of the 20th century turning France into a global power.

He first went to war during **World War I** and suffered several injuries, including a bullet to the knee and a bullet to his left hand. He was honored for his bravery after he would sneak across the trenches to eavesdrop on the German soldiers. De Gaulle was eventually caught by the Germans and made a prisoner of war. He made a total of five unsuccessful escape attempts by either digging holes through the floor or walls of his cell, hiding in laundry baskets, or disguising himself as a nurse. He spent the next 32 months as a prisoner of war and was quite unhappy that he had missed out on the fighting.

After **World War I**, he felt strongly that the French military had to transition from relying on horses to focusing on armored vehicles and tanks. He was an excellent writer and a gifted speaker. He would give many talks on how to improve the French army.

Unfortunately, the French were not ready for the aggressive German attacks in 1939 and 1940. Nazi Germany was able to take control of Paris and most of northern France by June of 1940, forcing the French government to retreat to the south of France. This government became known as the **Vichy Government** and would become an ally of Nazi Germany.

Charles de Gaulle moved to England in June of 1940 because he didn't accept the **submission** of France to Germany. He famously gave a speech on the radio on June 18, 1940, insisting that France would fight on. This was the beginning of the famous **French Resistance**.

He spent the rest of **World War II** coordinating the French Resistance. Despite having a **strained** relationship with U.S. president **Franklin Roosevelt** and British Prime Minister **Winston Churchill**, he pushed very hard for France to be controlled by the French after World War II.

Charles de Gaulle was very popular in France and even became President of France from 1958 to 1969. He insisted that France should be considered a world power. During his presidency, France developed nuclear weapons, becoming the world's fourth nuclear power after the U.S., the Soviet Union and Great Britain.

He resigned in 1969 and died a year later at the age of 80.

Submission: allowing a superior or stronger force to take control.

Strained: tired and difficult relationship.

1. What was Charles De Gaulle's nickname?

2. What was the name of the French government that controlled southern France in World War II, as allies of the Nazis?

3. Is France a nuclear power?

Brain Spark:

1. What is the name of the sterilization process for dairy products and eggs that significantly reduces the number of bacteria in them?

2. What city hosted the 1972 Summer Olympics, infamously known as the site of a terrorist attack that killed Israeli athletes?

3. Theranos entered into a partnership with what major pharmacy chain?

4. Charles Lindbergh landed in what European city to complete his trans-Atlantic flight in 1927?

JOAN OF ARC

Can a 16-year-old with visions from God lead a country into battle? In the 21st century, probably not. But in 1429? Sure!

Joan of Arc was born in **France** during a seemingly never-ending war between England and France known as the **Hundred Years' War**. As a teenager, Joan started announcing that she was having visions from God. Those visions included that she was going to lead France to victory in battle over **England** and help **Charles VII** assert his role as king over all of the French lands. At the time, King Charles's father had replaced him with **Henry V** of England as the heir to the French throne, leaving young Charles VII without a kingdom to rule.

Joan of Arc asked to lead his army. Despite her only being 16 years old, Charles agreed. With her hair cut short to look like a boy, she led the French army to a victory over England at the **Battle of Orleans**.

With the support of the French people, and after eight more successful battle victories over the English, she led Charles VII to the city of **Reims,** where he was officially crowned the King of France.

Some time later, Joan of Arc was captured by the English. The English were keen on having her renounce her visions and charged her with **heresy**. She refused to denounce her visions. The English had her burned at the stake. She was only 19 years old at the time.

Heresy: an opinion that goes against normally accepted religious teachings of the time.

1. What long-lasting war between France and England saw Joan of Arc lead troops into battle?
2. What French king was crowned king with the help of Joan of Arc?
3. Joan of Arc led French troops to victory over England in what famous battle?
4. In what city was Charles VII crowned king of France?

Brain Spark:

1. What very tall Frenchman was a leader of the French resistance against the Nazis in World War II?
2. According to legend, Nero played what instrument while Rome burned?
3. What President fired Douglas MacArthur from his role in the Korean War?
4. What was the location of the 1985 Soviet nuclear power plant disaster?

PABLO ESCOBAR

Pablo Escobar was the wealthiest criminal ever. By the time of his death, at age 44 in 1993, he was worth an estimated $30 billion dollars.

Escobar started off with small crimes in his home country of **Colombia.** At first, he was selling illegal cigarettes before moving on to stealing cars. Eventually he moved onto kidnapping people and holding them for **ransom**. He later transitioned to selling cocaine. He really gained **notoriety** when he established the **Medellin Cartel** (Medellin was the name of the town in Colombia where Escobar founded the cartel).

The Medellin Cartel made their millions by smuggling cocaine into the United States in the 1980s and 1990s. At one point, they were smuggling enough drugs around the world that they were generating $60 million per day.

Escobar and the Medellin Cartel **bribed** many officials. When that didn't work, they would threaten government officials and police. Escobar didn't shy away from ordering hitmen to murder anyone in his way. It is estimated that over 500 police officers were murdered, as well as thousands of government officials and their family members.

When Escobar had a Colombian presidential candidate and a justice minister murdered, the government pursued him more aggressively. He agreed to surrender on the conditions that he wouldn't be sent to the United States, that he could stay in a prison that he designed and built, and that he could even choose his own guards.

The prison was known as **La Catedral**. It had a soccer area, several waterfalls, Jacuzzis and other luxury amenities. He escaped the prison a year later, because he was concerned that the government would move him to a real prison.

The Colombian government hunted him down with the assistance of the U.S. government. When they eventually found him, he died in a hail of bullets.

Cartel: a group of suppliers that control the price of their product, by keeping the price at a high level and restricting competition. Most commonly referring to those who sell and distribute illegal drugs or weapons.

Bribed: persuade someone to behave in a certain way, usually by giving them money.

Ransom: a sum of money that is paid to release someone held against their will.

Notoriety: famous or well-known for bad behavior.

1. In what country did Pablo Escobar become a criminal?

2. In what city did Pablo Escobar start his criminal empire?

Brain Spark:

1. What was the name of the teenage girl who led France to nine battle victories over England during the Hundred Years' War?

2. Who developed the first vaccine for rabies?

3. Ayatollah Khomeini issued a "fatwa" for the death of what author?

4. What racist laws targeted African Americans in the United States in the 19th and 20th Centuries?

NOAM CHOMSKY

Noam Chomsky is considered the "Father of Modern Linguistics". **Linguistics** is the study of language and its structure. Chomsky developed and expanded the concept of "Transformational and Universal Grammar". Specifically, this is the idea that, across all languages around the world, there is a biological guidance that leads us to have nouns and verbs.

Noam Chomsky started off at the University of Pennsylvania and made his way to Harvard and then on to **M.I.T.** (**Massachusetts Institute of Technology**) where he spent most of his career. He has received many **honorary degrees** from universities around the world for his work on language and linguistics.

However, he is even more famous because of his strong anti-war activism. He was against the U.S. involvement in **Vietnam** and wrote a well-known essay, *"The Responsibility of Intellectuals"*, criticizing the U.S. government. He was arrested a few times because of his anti-war protests, and even made it on **President Richard Nixon's** "enemies list". He continued to pursue anti-war protests and was also against the U.S. invasion of Iraq in 2003. He is also an anti-capitalist and favors libertarian socialism (a concept of worker led production with minimal power given to managers, owners, or other authority figures).

Honorary degree: an honorary degree is given by a university to honor someone's achievements, although they may not have attended that school.

1. Who is known as the "Father of Modern Linguistics"?
2. Noam Chomsky famously protested the U.S. involvement in which war?
3. Noam Chomsky was on which U.S. president's "enemies list"?

Brain Spark:

1. What word describes "a group of suppliers that control the price of their product", commonly associated with the crimes of Pablo Escobar?
2. What was the name of the French government that allied with the Nazis during World War II?
3. What was the name of the movement for the liberation of Palestine?
4. What South African President released Nelson Mandela from prison in 1990?

AMELIA EARHART

Did you know that perhaps the most famous female pilot of all time disappeared on her last flight, and no one is sure where she died?

Born in **Kansas** in 1897, Amelia Earhart initially gained fame as the first **female** **aviator** to fly by herself (solo) across the **Atlantic Ocean** in 1932, at the age of 34. She was also the first pilot to accomplish several other solo flights, including from Hawaii to California.

After these successes, she attempted in 1937 to fly around the world. Although this had been accomplished by other pilots, her trip would have been special because it was to be the longest route around the world (along the **equator**). She spent a lot of time planning, including finding the right navigator for her flight. In 1937, navigators would rely on landmarks, as well as the positions of the sun, moon and stars. They didn't have GPS devices back then. Even the best navigators could be several miles off course with their estimations.

Amelia Earhart was able to fly around almost the entire world. However, the most challenging part was the flight across the Pacific Ocean. Because the Pacific is so vast, she had to carry extra fuel, and she also had to plan to land on small islands to refuel. Unfortunately, somewhere between **Indonesia** and **Hawaii**, she started to run out of fuel while looking for the right island to land on. Radio contact with the plane was lost and her disappearance became a **mystery**. While there are many theories as to what happened to her, the most likely is that she ran out of fuel and crashed in the ocean. Many attempts have been made to find her plane, but so far no one has been successful.

Aviator: pilot.

Equator: an imaginary line that divides the Earth into a Northern and Southern Hemisphere.

1. What state was Amelia Earhart born in?
2. In 1932, what ocean did Amelia Earhart fly across, becoming the first woman to do so?
3. What ocean was Amelia Earhart flying over when she disappeared in 1937?

Brain Spark:

1. Who is considered the "Father of Modern Linguistics"?
2. Joan of Arc led French troops to victory in what famous battle?
3. What is the term for the belief that a Jewish state should be established and maintained in Israel?
4. According to legend, Marie Antoinette said "Let them eat ____" when told that peasants had no more bread to eat?

STEPHEN HAWKING

We all know YOU are brilliant - that's why you are reading this book!!! But sometimes there are people so brilliant that people start to use them as examples of being super smart. You may have heard folks call smart people "Einstein". Well, a similar thing happened with **Stephen Hawking,** one of the most brilliant minds since Albert Einstein.

Hawking was a **physicist** and a **cosmologist**. Some of his biggest and most notable findings concerned **black holes**. He developed the black hole area theory, stating that the surface area of a black hole can never shrink.

Born in 1942 in England, Hawking was diagnosed with a **crippling** (and typically deadly) disease at the young age of 21. The disease is known as **A.L.S., or Lou Gehrig's Disease**. Over the following years, the disease left him unable to move most of his muscles and forced him to communicate using a computer as his voice. This disease did not stop him from becoming world famous for his theoretical physics ideas. He was widely considered among the smartest people on the planet.

Hawking's most famous book, ***A Brief History of Time***, was published in 1988 and has sold over 10 million copies.

Cosmologist: someone who studies the universe, how it forms, and how it behaves.

Crippling: causing someone to be unable to walk or move.

Black hole: a region in space where gravity is so strong that nothing (not even light) can escape. It usually occurs after a massive star dies and explodes.

1. Stephen Hawking suffered from what crippling disease?
2. What is the name of Stephen Hawking's most famous book?

Brain Spark:

1. Who became the first woman aviator to fly across the Atlantic Ocean?
2. What is the name of the famous, and incredibly wealthy, cartel leader from Colombia?
3. Nero was the leader of what empire?
4. What famous Supreme Court case found that segregation in schools was unconstitutional?

RAY KROC

Have you ever had a Happy Meal? How about Chicken McNuggets? Well, one man is responsible for these items being sold all over the world.

Ray Kroc is best known for expanding **McDonald's** fast-food restaurants into a fast-food empire. After World War II, Ray Kroc was selling milkshake mixing machines and met the McDonald brothers in **California**. The McDonald brothers had developed a system to make burgers quickly and had already built eight restaurants in California. Ray Kroc joined their team and expanded McDonald's to many other places in the United States and around the world.

Ray Kroc helped grow McDonald's through a **franchise** model. McDonald's would own the land and a local businessperson would become a **franchisee** by promising to closely follow all of McDonald's' rules. That way the ingredients, the customer service and the look of the restaurant would be the same no matter where you went.

The McDonald brothers weren't too happy with the way Ray Kroc was growing the business. They eventually sold their business to him for $1 million each in 1961 (which would be just under $9 million in 2021 dollars).

Ray Kroc's business model was a successful one, and very soon other fast-food chains would copy his franchise concept (Burger King, KFC, Arby's, etc.). By the time of his death in 1983, he had opened 7,500 McDonald's franchises and was worth over $600 million ($1.5 billion in 2021 dollars).

Franchise: a business with a specific method of distributing items and that maintains a trademark and business system (for example, McDonald's or Burger King).

Franchisee: a person who owns a franchise, typically paying a royalty or fee to use the trademark and business system.

1. In what state did the McDonald brothers first start McDonald's?

2. Who bought the McDonald's company from the McDonald brothers, and made billions of dollars expanding it all over the world?

Brain Spark:

1. What is the name of a space object that is so massive that not even light can escape from it?

2. Noam Chomsky famously protested the U.S. involvement in what 1960s war?

3. What is the term for the scientific study of germs?

4. Fill in the blank: Joseph Welch famously challenged Joseph McCarthy by asking him "Have you no sense of _________?"

HOWARD HUGHES

Have you ever heard of the word "**eccentric**"? Eccentric means a person who exhibits strange and odd behaviors. Of course, there are eccentric people everywhere. When it comes to famous people, there was perhaps no one more eccentric than **Howard Hughes.**

Howard Hughes made millions of dollars in the early 20th century after taking over his father's oil drilling company, and quickly started spending the money on his different interests. First, in the 1920s, Hughes showed great interest in movie making. He poured tons of money into making **extravagant** movies. He had a huge impact on the movie industry, even owning a movie studio for a while.

All the while, Hughes's interest in **aviation** was growing. In 1932, Hughes founded the Hughes Aircraft Company, and became obsessed with setting air speed records. The **Hughes Aircraft Company** began producing planes.

His most famous attempt at plane production came with the ***Spruce Goose***. *The Spruce Goose* was intended to be a giant plane, the largest ever made, that would be used to transport materials overseas during **World War II**. *The Spruce Goose* was huge. It was over five stories high, was mostly made of wood, and had a wingspan longer than an American football field. And it was costing the U.S. government millions, as they paid the Hughes Aircraft Company to build it.

The plane was a disaster. It was not finished until 1947, two years after **World War II** ended. It only flew once, reaching a height of 70 feet for 26 seconds.

Afterwards, Hughes became more and more eccentric. He began shutting himself off from most other people. He had also developed odd habits and rituals. In 1948, Hughes entered a room he had built to watch movies. He stayed in that dark room for four months, never leaving, and surviving on milk and chocolate, while using bottles as toilets.

In the 1960s, Hughes stayed in a hotel room at the Desert Inn, in **Las Vegas**. When the hotel asked him to leave so they could provide the room to gamblers, he bought the hotel. When a neon light from the nearby Sands Hotel was bothering him, he bought that hotel too, so that he could have the light removed. When he was convinced that a reporter was photographing him from the nearby Silver Slipper casino, he bought that one too, and had it boarded up.

Hughes's eccentricity was likely a result of mental illness. As he got older, his behaviors became stranger. By the time he died in 1976, he weighed only 90 lbs. (despite being 6 feet and 4 inches tall), was poorly groomed, and was living under an **alias**.

Hughes's life has been the subject of much interest. Most notably, it was featured in the 2004 movie ***The Aviator***, starring **Leonardo DiCaprio** as Howard Hughes.

Alias: a false or assumed name or identity.

Eccentric: unusual and strange behaviors.

Extravagant: spending a lot of money without much self-control.

Aviation: flying an airplane.

1. What was the name of the extremely large plane that Howard Hughes worked on, although it only flew once?
2. Howard Hughes had a big impact on which two industries?
3. What was the name of the 2004 movie about Howard Hughes, starring Leonardo DiCaprio?

Brain Spark:

1. Ray Kroc purchased what fast food restaurant, turning it into a massive nationwide success?
2. What state was Amelia Earhart born in?
3. What was the "vegetable" nickname of Charles de Gaulle?
4. Elizabeth Holmes famously wore what type of shirt at all times while leading her company Theranos?

BOBBY FISCHER

It's hard to believe today, at a time when the sports world is dominated by soccer, basketball and football champions, that years ago one of the most famous figures in American sports was a chess player. It's true!

Bobby Fischer was a **prodigy** at chess. In 1958, at the age of 14, he became the youngest U.S. chess champion ever. Fischer quickly grew into a phenomenon, and he reached his peak at the age of 29, when he defeated world chess champion **Boris Spassky** (from the Soviet Union) to become the first and only American **world chess champion** of the 20th century. This match was closely watched around the world as it occurred at the height of the Cold War and was dubbed the "Match of the Century". It was a huge surprise and shock to the world that a young American could beat a Soviet Chess Master, especially since the Soviets had dominated chess matches for the previous 25 years.

Soon, Fischer was all over television, magazines and newspapers. He was on the cover of *Sports Illustrated, Life Magazine, Time Magazine* and *Newsweek.* However, after his 1972 title-winning match against

Spassky, he seemingly disappeared. Fischer did not play another competitive public chess match again for twenty years.

Sadly, Fischer's disappearance from the public eye appeared to be partially related to his alleged struggles with mental illness. Fischer began to support strange **conspiracy theories** and began to speak of his vile **anti-Semitic** views.

After his successful 1992 rematch against Spassky, he faded again out of the public eye. He would episodically resurface with reports of strange behaviors and controversial views. He died in 2008.

His legend lives on, as his name is often used to refer to anyone who is a chess prodigy.

Prodigy: a young person with exceptional abilities.

Conspiracy Theory: a wild unproven belief that some secret organization or force is responsible for an event.

Anti-Semitic: prejudice against Jewish people.

1. What board game did Bobby Fischer play to become the youngest ever U.S. champion?

2. What Soviet chess champion did Bobby Fischer famously defeat in 1972?

Brain Spark:

1. What was the name of Howard Hughes's massive wood plane?

2. Stephen Hawking suffered from what disease?

3. Joan of Arc fought to help which French king be crowned King of France?

4. Douglas MacArthur studied at what New York military academy?

About the Authors

Dr. Michael Harwood graduated from Brown Medical School and is a board-certified Dermatologist. He is also a former Jeopardy! contestant. In addition to spending time with his two boys, he enjoys the piano, golf and writing.

Dr. Adrian Hamburger is a Harvard-trained Anesthesiologist and Pain Specialist, and dedicated father to two teenagers. He loves trivia, skiing, snorkeling, and chasing after his two dogs.

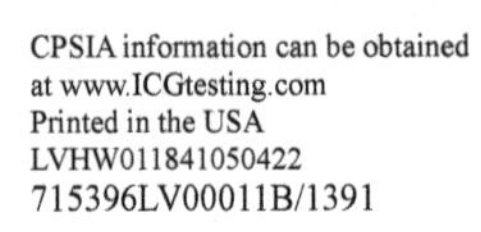

CPSIA information can be obtained
at www.ICGtesting.com
Printed in the USA
LVHW011841050422
715396LV00011B/1391